aran knits

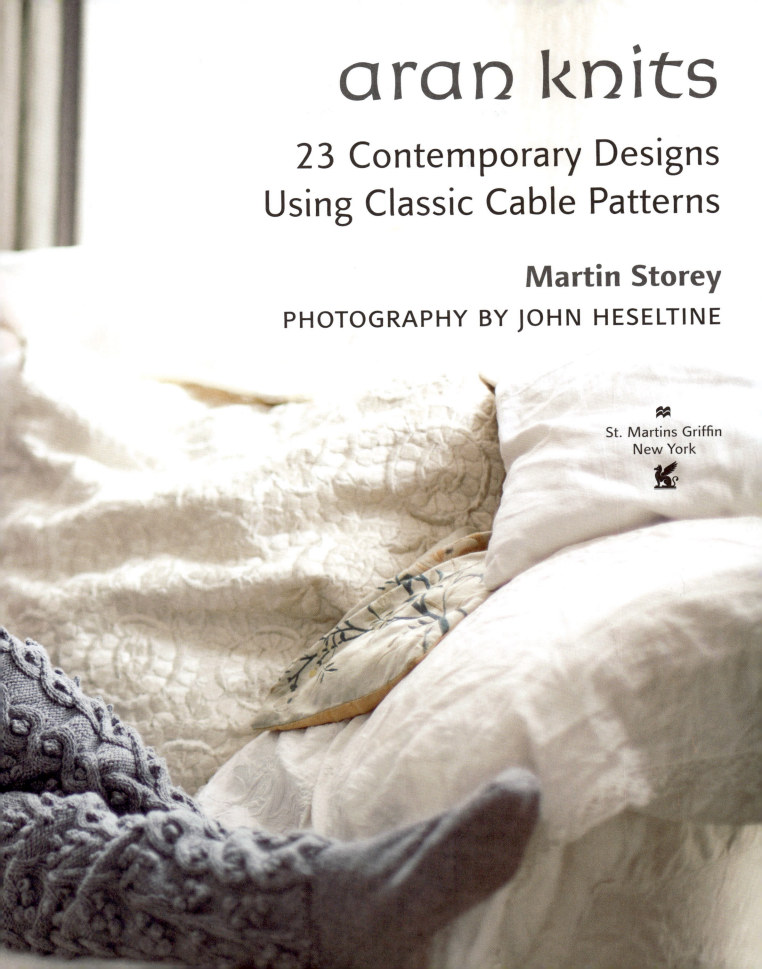

aran knits

23 Contemporary Designs
Using Classic Cable Patterns

Martin Storey

PHOTOGRAPHY BY JOHN HESELTINE

St. Martins Griffin
New York

Aran Knits

Copyright © 2012 by Berry & Bridges Ltd.

All rights reserved. Printed in Singapore.
For information, address St. Martin's Press,
175 Fifth Avenue, New York, N.Y. 10010.

www.stmartins.com

The written instructions, photographs, designs,
patterns, and projects in this volume are
intended for personal use of the reader and
may be reproduced for that purpose only.

Library of Congress Cataloging-in-Publication
Data Available Upon Request

ISBN 978-0-312-64221-1

First U.S. Edition: February 2012

10 9 8 7 6 5 4 3 2 1

Editor Katie Hardwicke
Designer Anne Wilson
Styling Susan Berry & Martin Storey
Pattern writer Penny Hill
Pattern checker Marilyn Wilson
Diagrams Lisa Richardson
Stills photographs Ed Berry (pp 4 [left],
5 [right], 18, 35, 38, 66, 70 [right: top, center,
and bottom], 73, 76 [center], 82, 86 [center],
91, 104, 110 [right: top, center, and bottom],
118, 128)
Publisher Susan Berry

contents

introduction

I have always loved working with, and creating, Aran and cable textures. I am particularly influenced by the cable and Aran stitches you find on the ganseys of traditional fishermen's sweaters around the British Isles. Many years ago, very early in my knitting career, I came across a wonderful book in a secondhand bookstore: Gladys Thompsons' *Patterns for Guernseys, Jerseys and Arans* (published in 1971 by Dover Publications). It was the beginning of my passion for all things Aran, and has proved to be very influential on my design.

For *Aran Knits* I have translated some of my favorite classic cable and Aran stitches into more contemporary silhouettes. I have also tried to keep the designs relatively simple. The patterns are created with those knitters in mind who want to experience the delight of creating Aran textures without finding them too complicated to knit.

Precisely because this book is primarily about texture, I have kept the colors to a soft and neutral palette, with highlights of lime and indigo. Some of the designs have even been knitted in the undyed British Sheep Breeds yarn (it is relatively new to Rowan, but has a quality that I particularly like).

My designs for the book fall into two groups—those for contemporary living (which we shot in a modern, pared down interior) and those for classic country (which we shot at a farmers' market and a quirky garden allotment). One of my great pleasures in doing these books lies in being part of the "team" that masterminds the photography shoots. Familiarity enables us to to work together in a very relaxed and informal atmosphere, which makes it fun, even though we have a lot to get through in the couple of days it takes to create the images. As you can see from the picture opposite, I am not allowed to gloat as the designer—even I get assigned to washing up duties!

This book is our third collaboration to date, and I love being involved in the whole process: sourcing locations, selecting the models, and working out the styling, and finally seeing it come to life on the page.

I hope this pleasure is reflected in the book we have created for you.

morag

This cropped top, with its big double or horseshoe cables, could work equally well worn as a warm wrap over a pretty dress or as a cozy cover-up with a shirt and jeans for a walk with the dog. It has quite a lot of "give" so the sizing is not too critical. Knitted in Rowan *Lima* yarn, which is primarily an alpaca/merino wool mix, it is lofty, soft, and light to wear.

MEASUREMENTS

S–M	M–L	L–XL	
To fit bust			
32–36	38–42	44–46	in
82–92	97–107	112–117	cm
Actual measurements			
Under bust			
30¾	39½	48½	in
78	100	123	cm
Length to shoulder			
15	16½	17¾	in
38	42	45	cm

YARN

9(11:13) x 1¾oz/109yd balls of Rowan *Lima* Titicaca 883

NEEDLES

Pair each of size 8 (5mm) and size 9 (5.5mm) knitting needles
Circular size 8 (5mm) needle
Cable needle

EXTRAS

Two buttons (1in/25mm diameter)

GAUGE

27 sts and 29 rows to 4in/10cm over patt using size 9 (5.5mm) needles *or size to obtain correct gauge.*

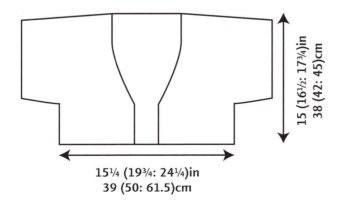

15¼ (19¾: 24¼)in
39 (50: 61.5)cm

15 (16½: 17¾)in
38 (42: 45)cm

ABBREVIATIONS

C6B—cable 6 back, slip next 3 sts on cable needle and hold at back of work, k3 then k3 from cable needle.
C6F—cable 6 front, slip next 3 sts on cable needle and hold at front of work, k3 then k3 from cable needle.
See also page 133.

BACK

Using size 9 (5.5mm) needles, cast on 92(118:144) sts.
Row 1 (rs) P2, [k10, p3] to last 12 sts, k10, p2.
Row 2 K2, [p10, k3] to last 12 sts, p10, k2.
Row 3 As row 1.
Row 4 K2, [p3, M1, p4, M1, p3, k3] to last 12 sts, p3, M1, p4, M1, p3, k2. *106(136:166) sts.*
Cont in cable patt.
Row 1 P2, [C6B, C6F, p3] to last 14 sts, C6B, C6F, p2.
Row 2 K2, [p12, k3] to last 14 sts, p12, k2.
Row 3 P2, [k12, p3] to last 14 sts, k12, p2.
Row 4 K2, [p12, k3] to last 14 sts, p12, k2.
Rows 5 to 8 Rep rows 3 and 4 twice.
These 8 rows form the patt and are repeated.
Work a further 4(6:8) rows.
Shape sleeves
* Cast on 7 sts at beg of next 2 rows, 8 sts at beg of foll 2 rows.
Rep from * once more. *166(196:226) sts.*
Work even until back measures 13(13¾:14½)in/ 33(35:37)cm from cast-on edge, ending with a wrong side row.
Shape upper sleeves and shoulders
** Bind off 7 sts at beg of next 2 rows, 8 sts at beg of foll 2 rows.
Rep from ** 2(3:4) times more.
Bind off 7 sts at beg of next 2 rows and 10(8:6) sts at beg of foll 2 rows. *42(46:50) sts.*
Bind off.
Mark center of bound-off edge with a colored thread.

LEFT FRONT

Using size 9 (5.5mm) needles, cast on 40(53:66) sts.
Row 1 (rs) P2, [k10, p3] to last 12 sts, k10, p2.
Row 2 K2, [p10, k3] to last 12 sts, p10, k2.

Row 3 As row 1.

Row 4 K2, [p3, M1, p4, M1, p3, k3] to last 12 sts, p3, M1, p4, M1, p3, k2. *46(61:76) sts.*

Cont in cable patt.

Row 1 P2, [C6B, C6F, p3] to last 14 sts, C6B, C6F, p2.

Row 2 K2, [p12, k3] to last 14 sts, p12, k2.

Row 3 P2, [k12, p3] to last 14 sts, k12, p2.

Row 4 K2, [p12, k3] to last 14 sts, p12, k2.

Rows 5 to 8 Rep rows 3 and 4 twice.

These 8 rows form the patt and are repeated.

Work a further 4(6:8) rows.

Shape sleeve

* **Next row** Cast on 7 sts, patt to end.

Next row Patt to end.

Next row Cast on 8 sts, patt to end.

Next row Patt to end.

Rep from * once more. *76(91:106) sts.*

Shape front neck

Next row Patt to last 2 sts, work 2 tog.

Work 3(5:7) rows.

Rep the last 4(6:8) rows once more.

Now dec one st at neck edge on next and every foll 4th row until 62(75:88) sts rem.

Work even until front measures the same as back to shoulder shaping, ending at armhole edge.

Shape upper sleeves and shoulders

** **Next row** Bind off 7 sts, patt to end.

Next row Patt to end.

Next row Bind off 8 sts, patt to end.

Next row Patt to end.

Rep from ** 2(3:4) times more.

Next row Bind off 7 sts, patt to end.

Next row Patt to end.

Bind off rem 10(8:6) sts.

RIGHT FRONT

Using size 9 (5.5mm) needles, cast on 40(53:66) sts.

Row 1 (rs) P2, [k10, p3] to last 12 sts, k10, p2.

Row 2 K2, [p10, k3] to last 12 sts, p10, k2.

Row 3 As row 1.

Row 4 K2, [p3, M1, p4, M1, p3, k3] to last 12 sts, p3, M1, p4, M1, p3, k2. *46(61:76) sts.*

Cont in cable patt.

Row 1 P2, [C6B, C6F, p3] to last 14 sts, C6B, C6F, p2.

Row 2 K2, [p12, k3] to last 14 sts, p12, k2.

Row 3 P2, [k12, p3] to last 14 sts, k12, p2.

Row 4 K2, [p12, k3] to last 14 sts, p12, k2.

Rows 5 to 8 Rep rows 1 and 2 twice.

These 8 rows form the patt and are repeated.

Work a further 5(7:9) rows.

Shape sleeve

Next row Cast on 7 sts, patt to end.

Next row Patt to end.

Next row Cast on 8 sts, patt to end.

Next row Patt to end.

Next row Cast on 7 sts, patt to end.

Next row Patt to end.

Next row Cast on 8 sts, patt to end.

Next row Work 2 tog, patt to end.

Work 3(5:7) rows.

Rep the last 4(6:8) rows once more.

Now dec one st at neck edge on next and every foll 4th row until 62(75:88) sts rem.

Work even until front measures the same as back to shoulder shaping, ending at armhole edge.

Shape upper sleeves and shoulders
** **Next row** Bind off 7 sts, patt to end.
Next row Patt to end.
Next row Bind off 8 sts, patt to end.
Next row Patt to end.
Rep from ** 2(3:4) times more.
Next row Bind off 7 sts, patt to end.
Next row Patt to end.
Bind off rem 10(8:6) sts.

LEFT NECK EDGE AND COLLAR

Join upper sleeve and shoulder seams.
With right side facing, using size 8 (5mm) needles cast on one st, pick up and k13(15:17) sts across back neck from colored thread to shoulder, 80(84:88) sts down neck edge to beg of neck shaping, 16(18:20) sts to cast-on edge. *110(118:126) sts.*
Row 1 (ws) P2, [k2, p2] to end.
This row sets the rib.
Shape for Collar
Next 2 rows Rib 22, turn, rib to end.
Next 2 rows Rib 28, turn, rib to end.
Next 2 rows Rib 34, turn, rib to end.
Next 2 rows Rib 40, turn, rib to end.
Cont in this way working 6 more sts on every right side row until 88(94:100) sts have been worked into collar, ending with a wrong side row.
Work 21(23:25) rows across all sts.
Using a size 9 (5.5mm) needle, bind off in rib.

RIGHT NECK EDGE AND COLLAR

With right side facing, using size 8 (5mm) needles pick up and k16(18:20) sts to beg of neck shaping, 80(84:88) sts up neck edge to shoulder, 13(15:17) sts across back neck to colored thread, cast on one st. *110(118:126) sts.*
Work in rib as given for left neck edge and Collar.
Shape for Collar
Next 2 rows Rib 22, turn, rib to end.
Next 2 rows Rib 28, turn, rib to end.
Next 2 rows Rib 34, turn, rib to end.
Next 2 rows Rib 40, turn, rib to end.

Cont in this way working 6 more sts on every wrong side row until 88(94:100) sts have been worked into collar, ending with a right side row.
Work 3 rows across all sts.
Buttonhole row 1 Rib 6, p2tog, y2o skp, rib to end.
Buttonhole row 2 Rib to end, working twice into y2o.
Work 12(14:16) rows across all sts.
Buttonhole row 1 Rib 6, p2tog, y2o skp, rib to end.
Buttonhole row 2 Rib to end, working twice into y2o.
Work 3 rows across all sts.
Using a size 9 (5.5mm) needle, bind off in rib.

SLEEVE BANDS

With right side facing, using size 8 (5mm) needles pick up and k102(110:118) sts evenly along row ends.
Row 1 P2, [k2, p2] to end.
Row 2 K2, [p2, k2] to end.
Rep the last 2 rows 7 times more and row 1 again.
Bind off in rib.

FINISHING

Join row-ends of Collar. Join side and underarm seams.
Sew on buttons.

moira

This scarf is super-long and has lots of character. The big wrapped cabled "knots" are really distinctive and are worked by knitting separate extensions and then wrapping the extensions around each other. This requires some patience, but the final result is wonderfully three-dimensional. It would make an ideal project for someone wanting to develop their basic cable skills. Knitted in *Lima*, like Morag on page 8, it would also look great in the same soft green (Titicaca, 883) or in duck-egg blue (Aztec, 894).

FINISHED SIZE

9in/23cm wide by 76½in/194cm long.

YARN

10 x 1¾oz/109yd balls of Rowan *Lima* Peru 889

NEEDLES

Pair of size 9 (5.5mm) knitting needles

GAUGE

20 sts and 26 rows to 4in/10cm square over St st using size 9 (5.5mm) needles *or size to obtain correct gauge.*

26 sts and 23 rows to 4in/10cm square over patt (slightly stretched) using size 9 (5.5mm) needles *or size to obtain correct gauge.*

ABBREVIATIONS

MK—make knot over 15 sts, [k5, turn, p5, turn] 4 times, break yarn and leave these sts on first safety pin, slip next 5 sts, onto a holder, rejoin yarn to sts on left-hand needle, [k5, turn, p5, turn] 4 times, break yarn and leave these sts on second safety pin. Ensuring strips are not twisted, take first safety pin across front of work and slip sts from first safety pin back onto left-hand needle, slip center sts from holder back onto left-hand needle, now wrap the 5 sts on second safety pin around those of first strip by sliding the safety pin behind first strip, then from top to bottom, between the first strip and center sts and bringing it back up level with the other sts, slip these back onto left-hand needle, rejoin yarn and work across these sts thus: k5, p5, k5.

See also page 133.

SCARF

Using size 9 (5.5mm) needles, cast on 61 sts.
Row 1 (rs) P2, k5, p5, k5, p2, [k2, p2, k5, p5, k5, p2] twice.
Row 2 K2, p5, k5, p5, k2, [p2, k2, p5, k5, p5, k2] twice.
Rows 3 to 8 Rep rows 1 and 2 three times.

Row 9 P2, MK, p2, [k2, p2, MK, p2] twice.
Row 10 As row 2.
Rows 11 to 16 Rep rows 1 and 2 three times.
These 16 rows form the patt.
Cont in patt until scarf measures 76½in/194cm from cast-on edge, ending with a 16th row.
Bind off in patt.

bonnie

This edge-to-edge bolero style shrug has a real touch of
glamour, making it the perfect evening cover-up, as the many
beads in the centers of the Aran diamond cable patterns and
on the collar catch the light and add that special sparkle.
It works well over a pretty printed blouse or dress. Knitted in
Rowan's ever popular *Wool Cotton*, it has a firm texture that
helps the beads to show up well.

MEASUREMENTS

S	M	L	XL	
To fit bust				
32–34	36–38	40–42	44–46	in
82–87	92–97	102–107	112–117	cm
Actual measurements				
Bust				
35½	40	45	50½	in
90	102	114	128	cm
Length to shoulder				
16	17	17¾	18½	in
41	43	45	47	cm

YARN

7(8:9:10) x 1¾oz/123yd balls of Rowan *Wool Cotton*
Smalt 963

NEEDLES

Pair each of size 5 (3.75mm) and size 6 (4mm) knitting
needles
Circular size 5 (3.75mm) needle
Cable needle

EXTRAS

Small glass beads, approx 850 (1000:1200:1500)

GAUGE

29 sts and 34 rows to 4in/10cm over patt using size 6
(4mm) needles *or size to obtain correct gauge.*

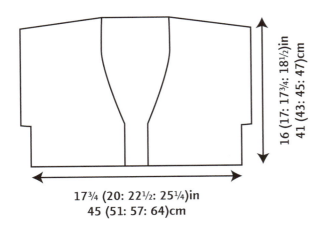

17¾ (20: 22½: 25¼)in
45 (51: 57: 64)cm

ABBREVIATIONS

C4B—cable 4 back, slip next 2 sts on cable needle and
hold at back of work, k2 then k2 from cable needle.
C5B—cable 5 back, slip next 3 sts on cable needle and
hold at back of work, k2 then k3 from cable needle.
Cr3R—cross 3 right, slip next st on cable needle and
hold at back of work, k2 then k1 from cable needle.
Cr3L—cross 3 left, slip next 2 sts on cable needle and
hold at front of work, k1 then k2 from cable needle.
Cr3Rp—cross 3 right purl, slip next st on cable needle
and hold at back of work, k2 then p1 from cable
needle.
Cr3Lp—cross 3 left purl, slip next 2 sts on cable
needle and hold at front of work, p1 then k2 from
cable needle.
B1—place bead, bring yarn to front of work, slip bead
up to next st, slip next st pw, take yarn to back.
Before commencing work, thread the beads onto 4
(4:5:5) balls of yarn and use for beading rows.
See also page 133.

BACK

Using size 5 (3.75mm) needles, cast on
109(125:141:157) sts.
Row 1 (rs) P1, [k3, p1] to end.
Row 2 K1, [p3, k1] to end.
Rep the last 2 rows 3 times more and row 1 again.
Inc row K1, p3, k1, M1, p3, M1, k1, p3, k1, [p2,
M1, p1, k1, p3, k1, M1, p3, M1, k1, p3, k1] to end.
129(148:167:186) sts.
Change to size 6 (4mm) needles.
Cont in cable patt.
Row 1 P4, Cr3R, k1, Cr3L, p4, [k4, p4, Cr3R, k1, Cr3L,
p4] to end.
Row 2 K4, p7, k4, [p4, k4, p7, k4] to end.
Row 3 P3, Cr3R, k1, B1, k1, Cr3L, p3, [C4B, p3, Cr3R,
k1, B1, k1, Cr3L, p3] to end.
Row 4 K3, p9, k3, [p4, k3, p9, k3] to end.
Row 5 P2, Cr3R, [k1, B1] twice, k1, Cr3L, p2, * k4, p2,
Cr3R, [k1, B1] twice, k1, Cr3L, p2; rep from * to end.
Row 6 K2, p11, k2, [p4, k2, p11, k2] to end.
Row 7 P2, k2, [k1, B1] 3 times, k3, p2, * C4B, p2, k2,

[k1, B1] 3 times, k3, p2; rep from * to end.

Row 8 As row 6.

Row 9 P2, Cr3Lp, [k1, B1] twice, k1, Cr3Rp, p2, * k4, p2, Cr3Lp, [k1, B1] twice, k1, Cr3Rp, p2; rep from * to end.

Row 10 As row 4.

Row 11 P3, Cr3Lp, k1, B1, k1, Cr3Rp, p3, [C4B, p3, Cr3Lp, k1, B1, k1, Cr3Rp, p3] to end.

Row 12 As row 2.

Row 13 P4, Cr3Lp, k1, Cr3Rp, p4, [k4, p4, Cr3Lp, k1, Cr3Rp, p4] to end.

Row 14 K5, p5, k5, [p4, k5, p5, k5] to end.

Row 15 P5, C5B, p5, [C4B, p5, C5B, p5] to end.

Row 16 K5, p5, k5, [p4, k5, p5, k5] to end.

These 16 rows form the patt and are repeated.

Cont in patt until back measures 6¾(7:7½:8)in/ 17(18:19:20)cm from cast-on edge, ending with a wrong side row.

Shape armhole

Row 1 Cast on 5 sts, p1, k4 across these sts, patt to end.

Row 2 Cast on 5 sts, k1, p4 across these sts, patt to end. *139(158:177:196) sts.*

Working extras sts into 4 st cable, work even until back measures 15(15¾:16½:17¼)in/38(40:42:44)cm from cast-on edge, ending with a wrong side row.

Shape upper arms and shoulders

Bind off 6(7:8:9) sts at beg of next 8 rows, 9(11:13:15) sts at beg of foll 2 rows and 10(12:14:16) sts at beg of next 2 rows.

Leave rem 53(56:59:62) sts on a spare needle.

LEFT FRONT

Using size 5 (3.75mm) needles, cast on 50(66:66:82) sts.

Row 1 (rs) [P1, k3] to last 6 sts, p1, k5.

Row 2 K2, [p3, k1] to end.

Rep the last 2 rows 3 times more and row 1 again.

Inc row K2, [p2, M1, p1, k1, p3, k1, M1, p3, M1, k1, p3, k1]. *59(78:78:97) sts.*

Change to size 6 (4mm) needles.

Cont in cable patt.

Row 1 [P4, Cr3R, k1, Cr3L, p4, k4] to last 2 sts, k2.

Row 2 K2, [p4, k4, p7, k4] to end.

Row 3 [P3, Cr3R, k1, B1, k1, Cr3L, p3, C4B] to last 2 sts, k2.

Row 4 K2, [p4, k3, p9, k3] to end.

Row 5 * P2, Cr3R, [k1, B1] twice, k1, Cr3L, p2, k4; rep from * to last 2 sts, k2.

Row 6 K2, [p4, k2, p11, k2] to end.

Row 7 * P2, k2, [k1, B1] 3 times, k3, p2, C4B; rep from * to last 2 sts, k2.

Row 8 As row 6.

Row 9 * P2, Cr3Lp, [k1, B1] twice, k1, Cr3Rp, p2, k4; rep from * to last 2 sts, k2.

Row 10 As row 4.

Row 11 [P3, Cr3Lp, k1, B1, k1, Cr3Rp, p3, C4B] to last 2 sts, k2.

Row 12 As row 2.

Row 13 [P4, Cr3Lp, k1, Cr3Rp, p4, k4] to last 2 sts, k2.

Row 14 K2, [p4, k5, p5, k5] to end.

Row 15 [P5, C5B, p5, C4B] to last 2 sts, k2.

Row 16 K2, [p4, k5, p5, k5] to end.

These 16 rows form the patt with garter-st border and are repeated.

Cont in patt until front measures 6¾(7:7½:8)in/ 17(18:19:20)cm from cast-on edge, ending with a wrong side row.

Shape armhole and front neck

Row 1 Cast on 5 sts, p1, k4 across these sts, patt to end. *64(83:83:102) sts.*

Next row Patt to end.

Working extras sts at side into 4-st cable, cont as foll:

Shape front neck

1st and 3rd sizes only

Next row Patt to last 8 sts, work 2 tog, patt 6.

Patt 2 rows.

Next row Patt 6, work 2 tog, patt to end.

Patt 2 rows.

2nd and 4th sizes only

Next row Patt to last 8 sts, work 2 tog, patt 6.

Patt 1 row.

All sizes

Rep the last 6(2:6:2) rows until 43(51:59:67) sts rem.

Work even until front measures the same as back to shoulder, ending at side edge.

Shape upper arm and shoulder

Bind off 6(7:8:9) sts at beg of next and 3 foll right side rows.

Patt 1 row.

Next row Bind off 9(11:13:15) sts, patt to end.

Patt 1 row.

Bind off rem 10(12:14:16) sts.

RIGHT FRONT

Using size 5 (3.75mm) needles, cast on 50(66:66:82) sts.

Row 1 (rs) K5, p1, [k3, p1] to end.

Row 2 K1, [p3, k1] to last 5 sts, p3, k2.

Rep the last 2 rows 3 times more and row 1 again.

Inc row [K1, p3, k1, M1, p3, M1, k1, p3, k1, p1, M1, p2] to last 2 sts, k2. *59(78:78:97) sts.*

Change to size 6 (4mm) needles.

Cont in cable patt.

Row 1 K2, [k4, p4, Cr3R, k1, Cr3L, p4] to end.

Row 2 [K4, p7, k4, p4] to last 2 sts, k2.

Row 3 K2, [C4B, p3, Cr3R, k1, B1, k1, Cr3L, p3] to end.

Row 4 [K3, p9, k3, p4] to last 2 sts, k2.

Row 5 K2, * k4, p2, Cr3R, [k1, B1] twice, k1, Cr3L, p2; rep from * to end.

Row 6 [K2, p11, k2, p4] to last 2 sts, k2.

Row 7 K2, * C4B, p2, k2, [k1, B1] 3 times, k3, p2; rep from * to end.

Row 8 As row 6.

Row 9 K2, * k4, p2, Cr3Lp, [k1, B1] twice, k1, Cr3Rp, p2; rep from * to end.

Row 10 As row 4.

Row 11 K2, [C4B, p3, Cr3Lp, k1, B1, k1, Cr3Rp, p3] to end.

Row 12 As row 2.

Row 13 K2, [k4, p4, Cr3Lp, k1, Cr3Rp, p4] to end.

Row 14 [K5, p5, k5, p4] to last 2 sts, k2.

Row 15 K2, [C4B, p5, C5B, p5] to end.

Row 16 [K5, p5, k5, p4] to last 2 sts, k2.

These 16 rows form the patt with garter-st border and are repeated.

Cont in patt until front measures 6¾(7:7½:8)in/ 17(18:19:20)cm from cast-on edge, ending with a right side row.

Shape armhole and front neck

Row 1 Cast on 5 sts, k1, p4 across these sts, patt to end. *64(83:83:102) sts.*

Working extras sts at side into 4-st cable, cont as foll:

Shape front neck

1st and 3rd sizes only

Next row Patt 6, work 2 tog, patt to end.

Patt 2 rows.

Next row Patt to last 8 sts, work 2 tog, patt 6.

Patt 2 rows.

2nd and 4th sizes only

Next row Patt 6, work 2 tog, patt to end.

Patt 1 row.

All sizes

Rep the last 6(2:6:2) rows until 43(51:59:67) sts rem. Work even until front measures the same as back to shoulder, ending at side edge.

Shape upper arm and shoulder

Bind off 6(7:8:9) sts at beg of next and 3 foll wrong side rows. Patt 1 row.

Next row Bind off 9(11:13:15) sts, patt to end.

Patt 1 row.

Bind off rem 10(12:14:16) sts.

NECK EDGE

Join shoulder seams.

With right side facing, using size 5 (3.75mm) needles, beg at neck shaping, pick up and k80(83:86:89) sts up right front neck edge, k53(56:59:62) sts from back neck, pick up and k81(84:87:90) sts down left front to beg of neck shaping. *214(223:231:241) sts.*

Row 1 (ws) K2, p3, [k1, p4, k1, p3] to last 2 sts, k2.

Row 2 K3, B1, k1, [p1, C4B, p1, k1, B1, k1] to last 2 sts, k2.

Row 3 As row 1.

Row 4 K5, [p1, k4, p1, k3] to last 2 sts, k2.

Rep the last 4 rows twice more and rows 1 and 2 again.

Next row K2, p3, [k1, p1, p2 tog, p1, k1, p3] to last 2 sts, k2. Bind off in patt.

SLEEVE BANDS

With right side facing, using size 5 (3.75mm) needles, pick up and k101(105:109:113) sts between markers.

Working in k1, p3 rib as for lower back, work as foll:

Next 2 rows Rib to last 29 sts, turn.

Next 2 rows Rib to last 21 sts, turn.

Next 2 rows Rib to last 13 sts, turn.

Next 2 rows Rib to last 5 sts, turn.

Next row Rib to end. Bind off in rib.

FINISHING

Join side and underarm seams.

BONNIE

cora

This oh-so-elegant little jacket has a real touch of class. You can join the front with a brooch, fastened either just below the collar or at the bust. It has a very simple slightly cropped shape and a wonderfully rich, wide lattice pattern cabled border all around the edges and forming the collar and cuffs, too. If you knit this, you are also supporting a great yarn tradition: the yarn is Rowan *British Sheep Breeds DK* (undyed, from the Bluefaced Leicester sheep). The sheep look good in it too!

MEASUREMENTS

	S	M	L	XL	
To fit bust					
	32–34	36–38	40–42	44–46	in
	82–87	92–97	102–107	112–117	cm
Actual measurements					
Bust					
	37¾	41½	45	48½	in
	96	105	114	123	cm
Length to shoulder					
	19¾	20½	21¼	22	in
	50	52	54	56	cm
Sleeve length					
	17¼	17¾	18	18½	in
	44	45	46	47	cm

YARN

12(14:15:16) x 1¾oz/131yd balls of Rowan *British Sheep Breeds DK* Brown Bluefaced Leicester 781

NEEDLES

Pair each of size 5 (3.75mm) and size 6 (4mm) knitting needles
Circular size 6 (4mm) needle
Cable needle

EXTRAS

One brooch

GAUGE

22 sts and 30 rows to 4in/10cm square over St st using size 6 (4mm) needles *or size to obtain correct gauge.*

ABBREVIATIONS

Cr4R — cross 4 right, slip next 2 sts on a cable needle and leave at back of work, k2, then p2 from cable needle.
Cr4L — cross 4 left, slip next 2 sts on a cable needle and leave at front of work, p2, then k2 from cable needle.
C4B — cable 4 back, slip next 2 sts on a cable needle and leave at back of work, k2, then k2 from cable needle.
C4F — cable 4 front, slip next 2 sts on a cable needle and leave at front of work, k2, then k2 from cable needle.
See also page 133.

BACK

Using size 5 (3.75mm) needles, cast on

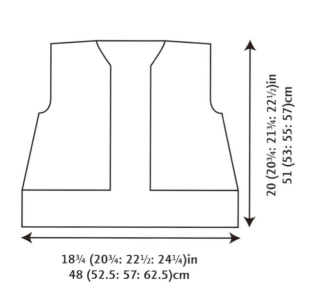

20 (20¾: 21¾: 22½)in
51 (53: 55: 57)cm

18¾ (20¾: 22½: 24¼)in
48 (52.5: 57: 62.5)cm

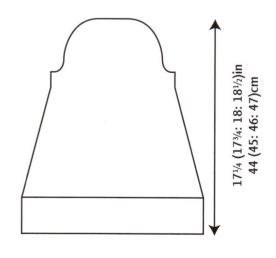

17¼ (17¾: 18: 18½)in
44 (45: 46: 47)cm

196(212:228:244) sts.

Row 1 P4, [C4B, p4] to end.

Row 2 K4, [p4, k4] to end.

Row 3 P2, [Cr4R, Cr4L] to last 2 sts, p2.

Row 4 K2, p2, k4, [p4, k4] to last 4 sts, p2, k2.

Row 5 P2, k2, p4, [C4F, p4] to last 4 sts, k2, p2.

Row 6 As row 4.

Row 7 P2, [Cr4L, Cr4R] to last 2 sts, p2.

Row 8 K4, [p4, k4] to end.

These 8 rows form the border patt.

Work a further 20 rows, ending row 4.

Dec row P2, k2, p1, p2tog, p1, * slip next 2 sts on a cable needle and leave at front of work, [slip next st from cable needle onto right-hand needle, k next st from left-hand needle, psso] twice, p1, p2tog, p1; rep from * to last 4 sts, k2, p2. *126(136:146:156) sts.*

Next row P to end.

Change to size 6 (4mm) needles.

Beg with a k row cont in St st.

Work 2 rows.

Dec row K9, skp, k to last 11 sts, k2tog, k9.

Work 5 rows.

Rep the last 6 rows 8 times more and the dec row again. *106(116:126:136) sts.*

Work even until back measures 12¼(12½:13:13½)in/ 31(32:33:34)cm from cast-on edge, ending with a p row.

Shape armholes

Bind off 7(8:9:10) sts at beg of next 2 rows. *92(100:108:116) sts.*

Next row K2, skp, k to last 4 sts, k2tog, k2.

Next row P to end.

Rep the last 2 rows 7(8:9:10) times more. *76(82:88:94) sts.*

Work even until back measures 19¾(20½:21¼:22)in/ 50(52:54:56)cm from cast-on edge, ending with a p row.

Shape shoulders

Bind off 6 sts at beg of next 4 rows and 6(7:8:9) sts at beg of foll 2 rows.

Leave 40(44:48:52) sts on a spare needle.

LEFT FRONT

Using size 5 (3.75mm) needles, cast on 116(124:140:148) sts.

Work 28 rows in patt as given for back, ending row 4.

Dec row P2, k2, p1, p2tog, p1, * slip next 2 sts on a cable needle and leave at front of work, [slip next st from cable needle onto right-hand needle, k next st from left-hand needle, psso] twice, p1, p2tog, p1; rep from * to last 36 sts, patt 36. *88(93:103:108) sts.*

Next row Patt 36, p to end.

Change to size 6 (4mm) needles.

Next row K to last 36 sts, patt 36.

Next row Patt 36, p to end.

These 2 rows form the St st with patt border.

Dec row K9, skp, k to last 36 sts, patt 36.

Work 5 rows.

Rep the last 6 rows 8 times more and the dec row again. *78(83:93:98) sts.*

Work even until front measures 12¼(12½:13: 13½)in/31(32:33:34)cm from cast-on edge, ending with a wrong side row.

Shape armhole

Next row Bind off 7(8:9:10) sts, patt to end. *71(75:84:88) sts.*

Work 1 row.

Next row K2, skp, k to last 36 sts, patt 36.

Next row Patt to end.

Rep the last 2 rows 7(8:9:10) times more. *63(66:74:77) sts.*

Work even until front measures 17¼(18:18½: 19¼)in/44(46:47:49)cm from cast-on edge, ending with a wrong side row.

Shape neck

Next row Patt to last 38(40:44:46) sts, turn and work on these sts. *25(26:30:31) sts.*

Next row Bind off 3(3:4:4) sts, p to end. *22(23:26:27) sts.*

Next row K to last 3 sts, k2tog, k1.

Next row P to end.

Rep the last 2 rows 3(3:5:5) times more. *18(19:20:21) sts.*

Work even until front measures the same as back to

shoulder, ending at armhole edge.

Shape shoulder

Bind off 6 sts at beg of next and foll right side row.

Work 1 row.

Bind off rem 6(7:8:9) sts.

RIGHT FRONT

Using size 5 (3.75mm) needles, cast on
116(124:140:148) sts.

Work 28 rows in patt as given for back, ending row 4.

Dec row Patt 36, p1, p2tog, p1, * slip next 2 sts on a
cable needle and leave at front of work, [slip next st
from cable needle onto right-hand needle, k next st
from left-hand needle, psso] twice, p1, p2tog, p1; rep
from * to last 4 sts, k2, p2. *88(93:103:108) sts.*

Next row P to last 36 sts, patt 36.

Change to size 6 (4mm) needles.

Next row Patt 36, k to end.

Next row P to last 36 sts, patt 36.

These 2 rows form the St st with patt border.

Dec row Patt 36, k to last 11 sts, k2tog, k9.

Work 5 rows.

Rep the last 6 rows 8 times more and the dec row
again. *78(83:93:98) sts.*

Work even until front measures 12¼(12½:13:13½)in/
31(32:33:34)cm from cast-on edge, ending with a right
side row.

Shape armhole

Next row Bind off 7(8:9:10) sts, p to last 36 sts, patt
71(75:84:88) sts.

Next row Patt 36, k to last 4 sts, k2tog, k2.

Next row Patt to end.

Rep the last 2 rows 7(8:9:10) times more.
63(66:74:77) sts.

Work even until front measures 17¼(18:18½:
19¼)in/44(46:47:49)cm from cast-on edge, ending
with a wrong side row.

Shape neck

Next row Patt 38(40:44:46) sts, leave these sts on a
holder, bind off 3(3:4:4) sts, k to end. *22(23:26:27) sts.*

Next row P to end.

Next row K1, skp, k to end.

Rep the last 2 rows 3(3:5:5) times more.
18(19:20:21) sts.

Work even until front measures the same as Back to
shoulder, ending at armhole edge.

Shape shoulder

Bind off 6 sts at beg of next and foll wrong side row.

Work 1 row.

Bind off rem 6(7:8:9) sts.

SLEEVES

With size 5 (3.75mm) needles, cast on
164(172:180:188) sts.

Work 28 rows in patt as given for back, ending row 4.

Dec row P2, k2, p1, p2tog, p1, * slip next 2 sts on a
cable needle and leave at front of work, [slip next st
from cable needle onto right-hand needle, k next st
from left-hand needle, psso] twice, p1, p2tog, p1; rep
from * to last 4 sts, k2, p2. *106(111:116:121) sts.*

P 1 row.

Change to size 6 (4mm) needles.

Beg with a p row cont in St st.

Work 3 rows.

Dec row K6, skp, k to last 8 sts, k2tog, k6.

Work 5 rows.

Rep the last 6 rows 14 times more and the dec row
again. *74(79:84:89) sts.*

Cont straight until sleeve measures 17¼(17¾:18:
18½)in/44(45:46:47)cm from cast-on edge, ending
with a p row.

Shape sleeve top

Bind off 7(8:9:10) sts at beg of next 2 rows.
60(63:66:69) sts.

Next row K2, skp, k to last 4 sts, k2tog, k2.

Next row P to end.

Rep the last 2 rows 8(9:10:11) times more.
42(43:44:45) sts.

Next row K2, skp, k to last 4 sts, k2tog, k2.

Work 3 rows

Rep the last 4 rows 3 times more. *34(35:36:37) sts.*

Next row K2, skp, k to last 4 sts, k2tog, k2.

Next row P to end.

Rep the last 2 rows once more. *30(31:32:33) sts.*

Bind off 3 sts at beg of next 4 rows.
Bind off.

COLLAR

Join shoulder seams.
With right side facing and size 6 (4mm) circular needle, slip 38(40:44:46) sts on right front holder onto needle, pick up and k27(26:27:26) sts up right side of front neck, k2, [M1, k2] 19(21:23:25) times across back neck sts, pick up and k26(25:26:25) sts down left side of front neck, patt across 38(40:44:46) sts on left front holder. *188(196:212:220) sts.*
Cont in patt as set by end sts.
Work in patt as set for 2¼in/6cm ending with row 3.
Change to size 5 (3.75mm) needles.
Work a further 1¼in/3cm, ending row 4.
Dec row P2, k2, p1, p2tog, p1, * slip next 2 sts on a cable needle and leave at front of work, [slip next st from cable needle onto right hand needle, k next st from left hand needle, psso] twice, p1, p2tog, p1; rep from * to last 4 sts, k2, p2.
Bind off as set.

FINISHING

Join side and sleeve seams. Set in sleeves. Secure front with brooch.

Fiona

This hat is great. It takes the famous, traditional Aran tasselled hat in a lace cable, bobble, and zig zag stitch and gives it a really fashionable twist, helped by the model wearing it slightly squashed and angled to one side rather than pulled down on her head. The result has real 1940s-style glamour. Knitted in beautifully soft Rowan *Baby Alpaca DK*, it takes just two balls. A great project to practice your textured stitches on!

FINISHED SIZE

To fit an average size head.

YARN

2 x 1¾oz/109yd balls of Rowan *Baby Alpaca DK* Southdown 208

NEEDLES

Pair of size 5 (3.75mm) knitting needles
Cable needle

GAUGE

24 sts and 32 rows to 4in/10cm over patt using size 5 (3.75mm) needles *or size to obtain correct gauge.*

ABBREVIATIONS

C4F—cable 4 front, slip next 2 sts on cable needle and leave at front of work, k2, then k2 from cable needle.
Cr2R—cross 2 right, slip next st on cable needle and leave at back of work, k1, then p1 from cable needle.
Cr2L—cross 2 left, slip next st on a cable needle and leave at front of work, p1, then k1 from cable needle.
MB—make bobble, [k1, p1, k1, p1, k1] all into next st, turn, p5, turn, k5, turn, p2tog, p1, p2tog, turn, sk2p.

MAIN PART

Using size 5 (3.75mm) needles, cast on 40 sts.
Row 1 (rs) K3, p2, k2, yo, k2tog, p2, k5, p5, [Cr2R] twice, p2, k5, p2, k2, yo, k2tog, p2.
Row 2 K2, p2, yo, p2tog, k2, p5, k3, [p1, k1] twice, k4, p5, k2, p2, yo, p2tog, k5.
Row 3 K3, p2, k2, yo, k2tog, p2, k2, MB, k2, p4, [Cr2R] twice, p3, k2, MB, k2, p2, k2, yo, k2tog, p2.
Row 4 K2, p2, yo, p2tog, k2, p5, k4, [p1, k1] twice, k3, p5, k2, p2, yo, p2tog, k5.
Row 5 K3, p2, k2, yo, k2tog, p2, k5, p3, [Cr2R] twice, p4, k5, p2, k2, yo, k2tog, p2.
Row 6 K2, p2, yo, p2tog, k2, p5, k5, [p1, k1] twice, k2, p5, k2, p2, yo, p2tog, k5.
Row 7 K3, p2, C4F, p2, k5, p2, [Cr2R] twice, p5, k5, p2, C4F, p2.
Row 8 K2, p2, yo, p2tog, k2, p5, k6, [p1, k1] twice, k1,
p5, k2, p2, yo, p2tog, k5.
Row 9 K3, p2, k2, yo, k2tog, p2, k5, p2, [Cr2L] twice, p5, k5, p2, k2, yo, k2tog, p2.
Row 10 As row 6.
Row 11 K3, p2, k2, yo, k2tog, p2, k2, MB, k2, p3, [Cr2L] twice, p4, k2, MB, k2, p2, k2, yo, k2tog, p2.
Row 12 As row 4.
Row 13 K3, p2, k2, yo, k2tog, p2, k5, p4, [Cr2L] twice, p3, k5, p2, k2, yo, k2tog, p2.
Row 14 As row 2.
Row 15 K3, p2, k2, yo, k2tog, p2, k5, p5, [Cr2L] twice, p2, k5, p2, k2, yo, k2tog, p2.
Row 16 K2, p2, yo, p2tog, k2, p5, k2, [p1, k1] twice, k5, p5, k2, p2, yo, p2tog, k5.
These 16 rows form the patt.
Work a further 144 rows. Bind off.

CROWN

With right side facing, using size 5 (3.75mm) needles, pick up and k 106 sts along left side. P 1 row.
Shaping
Row 1 [K6, k2tog] to last 2 sts, k2. *93 sts.*
Row 2 P to end.
Row 3 [K5, k2tog] to last 2 sts, k2. *80 sts.*
Row 4 P to end.
Row 5 [K4, k2tog] to last 2 sts, k2. *67 sts.*
Row 6 P to end.
Row 7 [K3, k2tog] to last 2 sts, k2. *54 sts.*
Row 8 P to end.
Row 9 [K2, k2tog] to last 2 sts, k2. *41 sts.*
Row 10 P to end.
Row 11 [K1, k2tog] to last 2 sts, k2. *28 sts.*
Row 12 P to end.
Row 13 [K2tog] to last 2 sts, k2. *15 sts.*
Row 12 P1, [p2tog] to end. *8 sts.*
Break off yarn, thread through rem sts, and fasten off.

FINISHING

Join seam. Using 18 strands of yarn, make a braid approx 4¾in/12cm long. Make a tassel approx 4in/10cm long, attach to end of braid. Attach to center of hat.

isla

Another exquisitely feminine soft shrug in a medallion seed stitch cable pattern with a deep rolled collar and brilliant deep curved welt; it really accentuates body shape while having lots of give. Like Cora on page 26, it is knitted in Rowan *British Sheep Breeds DK*, so it is both soft but has lots of substance. It looks good with soft prints, but would also dress up well, like Cora, with a formal cream shirt and a dark skirt or pants.

MEASUREMENTS

	S	M	L	XL	
To fit bust					
	32–34	36–38	40–42	44–46	in
	82–87	92–97	102–107	112–117	cm
Actual measurements					
Bust					
	35¾	42	48½	54½	in
	91	107	123	138	cm
Length to back neck					
	22	22	23½	23½	in
	56	56	60	60	cm
Sleeve length					
	18in/46cm				

YARN

12(13:14:15) x 1¾oz/131yd balls of Rowan *British Sheep Breeds DK*, Mid Brown Bluefaced Leicester 782

NEEDLES

Pair of size 6 (4mm) knitting needles
Circular size 3 (3.25mm) needle
Cable needle

GAUGE

22 sts and 30 rows to 4in/10cm square over St st using size 6 (4mm) needles *or size to obtain correct gauge.*

32 sts and 30 rows to 4in/10cm square over cable patt using size 6 (4mm) needles *or size to obtain correct gauge.*

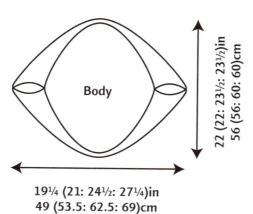

19¼ (21: 24½: 27¼)in
49 (53.5: 62.5: 69)cm

22 (22: 23½: 23½)in
56 (56: 60: 60)cm

ABBREVIATIONS

C8R—cross 8 right, slip next 4 sts on a cable needle and leave at back of work, [k1, p1] twice, then k4 from cable needle.

C8L—cross 8 left, slip next 4 sts on a cable needle and leave at front of work, k4, then [k1, p1] twice from cable needle.

See also page 133.

BACK

Using size 6 (4mm) needles, cast on 123(144:165:186) sts.

Row 1 (rs) * P3, k2, [k1, p1] 4 times, k2, p3, k3; rep from * to last 18 sts, p3, k2, [k1, p1] 4 times, k2, p3.

Row 2 * K3, p2, [p1, k1] 4 times, p2, k3, p3; rep from * to last 18 sts, k3, p2, [p1, k1] 4 times, p2, k3.

Row 3 (inc row) * P3, [k1, M1] twice, [k1, p1] 4 times, [M1, k1] twice, p3, k3; rep from * to last 18 sts, p3, [k1, M1] twice, [k1, p1] 4 times, [M1, k1] twice p3. *147(172:197:222) sts.*

Row 4 * K3, p4, [p1, k1] 4 times, p4, k3, p3; rep from * to last 22 sts, k3, p4, [p1, k1] 4 times, p4, k3.
Cont in patt.

Row 1 (rs) * P3, C8R, C8L, p3, k3; rep from * to last 22 sts, p3, C8R, C8L, p3.

Row 2 * K3, [p1, k1] twice, p9, k1, p1, k4, p3; rep from * to last 22 sts, k3, [p1, k1] twice, p9, k1, p1, k4.

Row 3 * P3, [k1, p1] twice, k9, p1, k1, p4, k3; rep

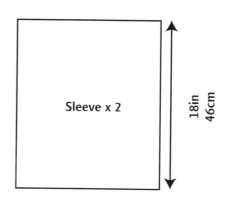

Sleeve x 2

18in
46cm

from * to last 22 sts, p3, [k1, p1] twice, k9, p1, k1, p4.

Row 4 * K3, [p1, k1] twice, p9, k1, p1, k4, p3; rep from * to last 22 sts, k3, [p1, k1] twice, p9, k1, p1, k4.

Rows 5 to 10 Rep rows 3 and 4 three times.

Row 11 * P3, C8L, C8R, p3, k3; rep from * to last 22 sts, p3, C8L, C8R, p3.

Row 12 * K3, p4, [p1, k1] 4 times, p4, k3, p3; rep from * to last 22 sts, k3, p4, [p1, k1] 4 times, p4, k3.

Row 13 * P3, k4, [k1, p1] 4 times, k4, p3, k3; rep from * to last 22 sts, p3, k4, [k1, p1] 4 times, k4, p3.

Row 14 * K3, p4, [p1, k1] 4 times, p4, k3, p3; rep from * to last 22 sts, k3, p4, [p1, k1] 4 times, p4, k3.

Rows 15 to 24 Rep rows 13 and 14 five times more. These 24 rows form the patt.

Work a further 96(96:106:106) rows, ending with row 24(24:10:10).

1st and 2nd sizes only

Row 1 dec (rs) * P3, slip next 4 sts on a cable needle and leave at back of work, [k1, p1] twice, then [k2tog] twice from cable needle, slip next 4 sts on a cable needle and leave at front of work, [k2tog] twice, then [k1, p1] twice from cable needle, p3, k3; rep from * to last 22 sts, p3, slip next 4 sts on a cable needle and leave at back of work, [k1, p1] twice, then [k2tog]

twice from cable needle, slip next 4 sts on a cable needle and leave at front of work, [k2tog] twice, then [k1, p1] twice from cable needle, p3. *123(144:–:–) sts.*

Row 2 * K3, [p1, k1] twice, p5, k1, p1, k4, p3; rep from * to last 18 sts, k3, [p1, k1] twice, p5, k1, p1, k4.

Row 3 * P3, [k1, p1] twice, k4, [k1, p1] twice, p3, k3; rep from * to last 18 sts, p3, [k1, p1] twice, k4, [k1, p1] twice, p3.

Row 4 * K3, [p1, k1] twice, p5, k1, p1, k4, p3; rep from * to last 18 sts, k3, [p1, k1] twice, p5, k1, p1, k4.

3rd and 4th sizes only

Row 1 dec (rs) * P3, slip next 4 sts on a cable needle and leave at front of work, [k2tog] twice, then [k1, p1] twice from cable needle, slip next 4 sts on a cable needle and leave at back of work, [k1, p1] twice, then [k2tog] twice from cable needle, p3, k3; rep from * to last 22 sts, p3, slip next 4 sts on a cable needle and leave at front of work, [k2tog] twice, then [k1, p1] twice from cable needle, slip next 4 sts on a cable needle and leave at back of work, [k1, p1] twice, then [k2tog] twice from cable needle, p3. *– (–:165:186) sts.*

Row 2 * K3, p2, [p1, k1] 4 times, p2, k3, p3; rep from * to last 18 sts, k3, p2, [p1, k1] 4 times, p2, k3.

Row 3 * P3, k2, [k1, p1] 4 times, k2, p3, k3; rep from * to last 18 sts, p3, k2, [k1, p1] 4 times, k2, p3.

Row 4 * K3, p2, [p1, k1] 4 times, p2, k3, p3; rep from * to last 18 sts, k3, p2, [p1, k1] 4 times, p2, k3.

All sizes

Border

Using circular size 3 (3.25mm) needle, k across 123(144:165:186) sts at top of back, with wrong sides together fold back in half, pick up and k123(144:165:186) sts across cast-on edge of back. *246(288:330:372) sts.*

Cont in rounds.

1st round [K1, M1, p1, M1] to end of round. *492(576:660:744) sts.*

2nd round [K2, p2] to end of round.

Rep the last round for 5½in/14cm.

Using a size 6 (4mm) needle, bind off in rib.

SLEEVES

Using size 6 (4mm) needles, cast on 102(102:123:123) sts.

Row 1 (rs) * P3, k2, [k1, p1] 4 times, k2, p3, k3; rep from * to last 18 sts, p3, k2, [k1, p1] 4 times, k2, p3.

Row 2 * K3, p2, [p1, k1] 4 times, p2, k3, p3; rep from * to last 18 sts, k3, p2, [p1, k1] 4 times, p2, k3.

Row 3 (inc row) * P3, [k1, M1] twice, [k1, p1] 4 times, [M1, k1] twice, p3, k3; rep from * to last 18 sts, p3, [k1, M1] twice, [k1, p1] 4 times, [M1, k1] twice, p3. *122(122:147:147) sts.*

Row 4 * K3, p4, [p1, k1] 4 times, p4, k3, p3; rep from * to last 22 sts, k3, p4, [p1, k1] 4 times, p4, k3.

Cont in patt.

Row 1 (rs) * P3, C8R, C8L, p3, k3; rep from * to last 22 sts, p3, C8R, C8L, p3.

Row 2 * K3, [p1, k1] twice, p9, k1, p1, k4, p3; rep from * to last 22 sts, k3, [p1, k1] twice, p9, k1, p1, k4.

These 2 rows set the patt.

Work a further 128 rows, ending with row 10.

Row 1 (dec) * P3, slip next 4 sts on a cable needle and leave at front of work, [k2tog] twice, then [k1, p1] twice from cable needle, slip next 4 sts on a cable needle and leave at back of work, [k1, p1] twice, then [k2tog] twice from cable needle, p3, k3; rep from * to last 22 sts, p3, slip next 4 sts on a cable needle and leave at front of work, [k2tog] twice, then [k1, p1] twice from cable needle, slip next 4 sts on a cable needle and leave at back of work, [k1, p1] twice, then [k2tog] twice from cable needle, p3. *102(102:123:123) sts.*

Row 2 * K3, p2, [p1, k1] 4 times, p2, k3, p3; rep from * to last 18 sts, k3, p2, [p1, k1] 4 times, p2, k3.

Row 3 * P3, k2, [k1, p1] 4 times, k2, p3, k3; rep from * to last 18 sts, p3, k2, [k1, p1] 4 times, k2, p3.

Row 4 * K3, p2, [p1, k1] 4 times, p2, k3, p3; rep from * to last 18 sts, k3, p2, [p1, k1] 4 times, p2, k3.

Bind off in patt.

FINISHING

Join sleeve seams. Sew in sleeves.

ISLA

berry

If you don't have the time for the Fiona hat on page 35, then knit this little headband. And if you have a little more time, why not try some of the other great designs all featuring the Berry motif of bobble trees and open cables with bobbles in their centers; they give you a chance to practice making little bobbles. Knitted in various shades of gray in Rowan *Wool Cotton*, you can choose from the headband, a vest, a beret, fingerless mittens, or cozy long socks. Or all of them, if you wish!

headband

FINISHED SIZE
To fit an average size head. Width 2¾in/7cm.

YARN
1 x 1¾oz/123yd ball of Rowan *Wool Cotton* Clear 941

NEEDLES
Pair of size 5 (3.75mm) knitting needles
Cable needle

GAUGE
29 sts and 32 rows to 4in/10cm square over patt using size 5 (3.75mm) needles *or size to obtain correct gauge.*

ABBREVIATIONS
Cr2R—cross 2 right, slip next st on a cable needle and leave at back of work, k1, then p1 from cable needle.
Cr2L—cross 2 left, slip next st on a cable needle and leave at front of work, p1, then k1 from cable needle.
Cr2Rtbl—cross 2 right, slip next st on a cable needle and leave at back of work, k1tbl, then k1tbl from cable needle.
Cr2Ltbl—cross 2 left, slip next st on a cable needle and leave at front of work, k1tbl, then k1tbl from cable needle.
MK—make knot, [k1, p1, k1, p1, k1] all in next st, turn, p5, turn, pass 2nd, 3rd, and 4th sts over the first st on left-hand needle, then k1tbl to complete the knot.
See also page 133.

HEADBAND
Using size 5 (3.75mm) needles, cast on 20 sts.
Row 1 K3, p5, Cr2Rtbl, k1, p3, Cr2L, MK, k3.
Row 2 K4, p1, k4, p3, k8.
Row 3 K3, p4, Cr2R, k2, p3, MK, Cr2L, k3.
Row 4 K3, p1, k5, p2, k1, p1, k7.
Row 5 K3, p2, MK, Cr2R, p1, k2, p5, MK, k3.
Row 6 K9, p2, k2, p1, k6.
Row 7 K3, p2, Cr2R, MK, p1, k2, p6, k3.
Row 8 K9, p2, k3, p1, k5.
Row 9 K3, MK, Cr2R, p3, k1, Cr2Ltbl, p5, k3.
Row 10 K7, p4, k4, p1, k4.
Row 11 K3, Cr2R, MK, p3, k2, Cr2L, p4, k3.
Row 12 K7, p1, k1, p2, k5, p1, k3.
Row 13 K3, MK, p5, k2, p1, Cr2L, MK, p2, k3.
Row 14 K6, p1, k2, p2, k9.
Row 15 K3, p6, k2, p1, MK, Cr2L, p2, k3.
Row 16 K5, p1, k3, p2, k9.
These 16 rows form the patt panel with garter-st edging.
Rep these 16 rows ten times more.
Bind off.

FINISHING
Join cast-on and bound-off edges.

BERRY

vest

MEASUREMENTS

	S	M	L	XL	
To fit bust					
	32–34	36–38	40–42	44–46	in
	82–87	92–97	102–107	112–117	cm
Actual measurements					
Bust					
	36¼	39½	44	48	in
	92	100	112	122	cm
Length to shoulder					
	23¾	24½	25¼	26	in
	60	62	64	66	cm

YARN

10(11:12:13) x 1¾oz/123yd balls of Rowan *Wool Cotton* Misty 903

NEEDLES

Pair each of size 3 (3.25mm) and size 5 (3.75mm) knitting needles
Circular size 3 (3.25mm) needle
Cable needle

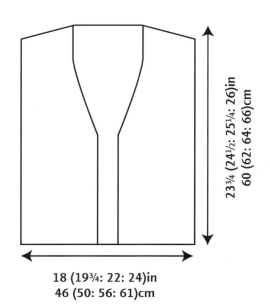

18 (19¾: 22: 24)in
46 (50: 56: 61)cm

23¾ (24½: 25¼: 26)in
60 (62: 64: 66)cm

EXTRAS

Six buttons (½in/15mm diameter)

GAUGE

23 sts and 32 rows to 4in/10cm square over St st using size 5 (3.75mm) needles *or size to obtain correct gauge.*
29 sts and 32 rows to 4in/10cm square over cable patt using size 5 (3.75mm) needles *or size to obtain correct gauge.*

ABBREVIATIONS

Cr2R—cross 2 right, slip next st on a cable needle and leave at back of work, k1, then p1 from cable needle.
Cr2L—cross 2 left, slip next st on a cable needle and leave at front of work, p1, then k1 from cable needle.
Cr2Rtbl—cross 2 right, slip next st on a cable needle and leave at back of work, k1tbl, then k1tbl from cable needle.
Cr2Ltbl—cross 2 left, slip next st on a cable needle and leave at front of work, k1tbl, then k1tbl from cable needle.
Cr4R—cross 4 right, slip next st on a cable needle and leave at back of work, k3, then p1 from cable needle.
Cr4L—cross 4 left, slip next 3 sts on a cable needle and leave at front of work, p1, then k3 from cable needle.
C7B—cable 7 back, slip next 4 sts on a cable needle and leave at back of work, k3, slip last st on cable needle back onto left-hand needle, p this st then k3 from cable needle.
MB—make bobble, [k1, p1, k1, p1, k1] all in next st, turn, p5, turn, k5, turn, p2tog, p1, p2tog, turn, sk2p to complete the bobble.
MK—make knot, [k1, p1, k1, p1, k1] all in next st, turn, p5, turn, pass 2nd, 3rd, and 4th sts over the first st on left-hand needle, then k1tbl to complete the knot.
See also page 133.

Patt Panel A (worked over 15 sts)
Row 1 P4, C7B, p4.
Row 2 K4, p3, k1, p3, k4.
Row 3 P3, C4R, p1, C4L, p3.
Row 4 K3, p3, k3, p3, k3.
Row 5 P2, C4R, p3, C4L, p2.
Row 6 K2, p3, k5, p3, k2.
Row 7 P2, k3, p2, MB, p2, k3, p2.
Row 8 K2, p3, k5, p3, k2.
Row 9 P2, C4L, p3, C4R, p2.
Row 10 K3, p3, k3, p3, k3.
Row 11 P3, C4L, p1, C4R, p3.
Row 12 K4, p3, k1, p3, k4.
These 12 rows form the patt panel A.

Patt Panel B (worked over 14 sts)
Row 1 P5, Cr2Rtbl, k1, p3, Cr2L, MK.
Row 2 K1, p1, k4, p3, k5.
Row 3 P4, Cr2R, k2, p3, MK, Cr2L.
Row 4 P1, k5, p2, k1, p1, k4.
Row 5 P2, MK, Cr2R, p1, k2, p5, MK.
Row 6 K6, p2, k2, p1, k3.
Row 7 P2, Cr2R, MK, p1, k2, p6.
Row 8 K6, p2, k3, p1, k2.
Row 9 MK, Cr2R, p3, k1, Cr2Ltbl, p5.
Row 10 K4, p4, k4, p1, k1.
Row 11 Cr2R, MK, p3, k2, Cr2L, p4.
Row 12 K4, p1, k1, p2, k5, p1.
Row 13 MK, p5, k2, p1, Cr2L, MK, p2.
Row 14 K3, p1, k2, p2, k6.
Row 15 P6, k2, p1, MK, Cr2L, p2.
Row 16 K2, p1, k3, p2, k6.
These 16 rows form the patt panel.

BACK

Using size 3 (3.25mm) needles, cast on
126(138:154:168) sts.
Row 1 (rs) P4(6:4:6), [k6, p8(9:8:9)] 1(1:2:2)
times, k6, p10(11:10:11), k2, p4, k1, p5(6:5:6), [k6,
p8(9:8:9)] twice, k6, p10(11: 10:11), k2, p4, k1,
p5(6:5:6), [k6, p8(9:8:9)] 1(1:2:2) times, k6, p4(6:4:6).
Row 2 K4(6:4:6), p6, [k8(9:8:9), p6] 1(1:2:2) times,

k5(6:5:6), p1, k4, p2, k10(11: 10:11), p6, [k8(9:8:9),
p6] twice, k5(6:5:6), p1, k4, p2, k10(11:10:11), p6,
[k8(9:8:9), p6] 1(1:2:2) times, k4(6:4:6).
Row 3 As row 1.
Row 4 K4(6:4:6), p3, M1, p3, [k8(9:8:9), p3, M1, p3]
1(1:2:2) times, k5(6:5:6), p1, k4, p2, k10(11: 10:11),
p3, M1, p3, [k8(9:8:9), p3, M1, p3] twice, k5(6:5:6),
p1, k4, p2, k10(11:10:11), p3, M1, p3, [k8(9:8:9), p3,
M1, p3] 1(1:2:2) times, k4(6:4:6).
133(145:163:177) sts.
Change to size 5 (3.75mm) needles and patt.
Row 1 P0(2:0:2), [work across 1st row Patt Panel A,
p0(1:0:1)] 2(2:3:3) times, work across 1st row Patt
Panel B, p0(1:0:1), [work across 1st row Patt Panel A,
p0(1:0:1)] 3 times, work across 1st row Patt Panel B,
[p0(1:0:1), work across 1st row Patt Panel A] 2(2:3:3)
times, p0(2:0:2).
Row 2 K0(2:0:2), [work across 2nd row Patt Panel A,
k0(1:0:1)] 2(2:3:3) times, work across 2nd row Patt
Panel B, k0(1:0:1), [work across 2nd row Patt Panel A,
k0(1:0:1)] 3 times, work across 2nd row Patt Panel B,
[k0(1:0:1), work across 2nd row Patt Panel A] 2(2:3:3)
times, k0(2:0:2).
These 2 rows set the patt.
Cont in patt until back measures 13¾(14¼:14½:
15)in/35(36:37:38)cm from cast-on edge, ending with
a wrong side row.
Mark each end of last row to denote beginning of
armhole.
Work even until back measures 22(22¾:23½:
24½)in/56(58:60:62)cm from cast-on edge, ending
with a wrong side row.
Shape shoulders
Bind off 6(6:7:7) sts at beg of next 10 rows and
8(10:11:13) sts at beg of foll 4 rows. *41(45:49:55) sts.*
Bind off.

LEFT FRONT

Using size 3 (3.25mm) needles, cast on 56(61:70:76)
sts.
Row 1 (rs) P4(6:4:6), [k6, p8(9:8:9)] 1(1:2:2) times,
k6, p10(11:10:11), k2, p4, k1, p5(6:5:6), k6, p4.

Row 2 K4, p6, k5(6:5:6), p1, k4, p2, k10(11:10:11), p6, [k8(9:8:9), p6] 1(1:2:2) times, k4(6:4:6).

Row 3 As row 1.

Row 4 K4, p3, M1, p3, k5(6:5:6), p1, k4, p2, k10(11:10:11), p3, M1, p3, [k8(9:8:9), p3, M1, p3] 1(1:2:2) times, k4(6:4:6). *59(64:74:80) sts.*

Change to size 5 (3.75mm) needles and patt.

Row 1 P0(2:0:2), [work across 1st row Patt Panel A, p0(1:0:1)] 2(2:3:3) times, work across 1st row Patt Panel B, p0(1:0:1), work across 1st row Patt Panel A.

Row 2 Work across 2nd row Patt Panel A, k0(1:0:1), work across 2nd row Patt Panel B, [k0(1:0:1), work across 2nd row Patt Panel A] 2(2:3:3) times, k0(2:0:2).

These 2 rows set the patt.

Cont in patt until front measures 11¾(12¼:12½: 13)in/30(31:32:33)cm from cast-on edge, ending with a wrong side row.

Shape front neck

Next row Patt to last 2 sts, work 2 tog.

Work 4 rows.

Next row Work 2 tog, patt to end.

Work 4 rows.

Rep the last 10 rows until 46(50:57:61) sts rem.

Work even until front measures the same as back to shoulder shaping, ending at side edge.

Shape shoulder

Bind off 6(6:7:7) sts at beg of next and 4 foll right side rows.

Work 1 row.

Bind off 8(10:11:13) sts at beg of next row.

Work 1 row.

Bind off rem 8(10:11:13) sts.

Place a marker at side edge to match back to denote beginning of armhole.

RIGHT FRONT

Using size 3 (3.25mm) needles, cast on 56(61:70:76) sts.

Row 1 (rs) P4, k6, p10(11: 10:11), k2, p4, k1, p5(6:5:6), [k6, p8(9:8:9)] 1(1:2:2) times, k6, p4(6:4:6).

Row 2 K4(6:4:6), p6, [k8(9:8:9), p6] 1(1:2:2) times, k5(6:5:6), p1, k4, p2, k10(11: 10:11), p6, k4.

Row 3 As row 1.

Row 4 K4(6:4:6), p3, M1, p3, [k8(9:8:9), p3, M1, p3] 1(1:2:2) times, k5(6:5:6), p1, k4, p2, k10(11: 10:11), p3, M1, p3, k4. *59(64:74:80) sts.*

Change to size 5 (3.75mm) needles and patt.

Row 1 Work across 1st row Patt Panel A, p0(1:0:1), work across 1st row patt panel B, [p0(1:0:1), work across 1st row patt panel A] 2(2:3:3) times, p0(2:0:2).

Row 2 K0(2:0:2), [work across 2nd row patt panel A, k0(1:0:1)] 2(2:3:3) times, work across 2nd row patt panel B, k0(1:0:1), work across 2nd row patt panel A.

These 2 rows set the patt.

Cont in patt until front measures 11¾(12¼:12½: 13)in/30(31:32:33)cm from cast-on edge, ending with a wrong side row.

Shape front neck

Next row Work 2 tog, patt to end.

Work 4 rows.

Next row Patt to last 2 sts, work 2 tog.

Work 4 rows.

Rep the last 10 rows until 46(50:57:61) sts rem.

Work even until front measures the same as back to shoulder shaping, ending at side edge.

Shape shoulder

Bind off 6(6:7:7) sts at beg of next and 4 foll wrong side rows.

Work 1 row.

Bind off 8(10:11:13) sts at beg of next row.

Work 1 row.

Bind off rem 8(10:11:13) sts.

Place a marker at side edge to match back to denote beginning of armhole.

FRONTBAND

Join shoulder seams.

With right side facing, using circular size 3 (3.25mm) needle, pick up and k71(74:76:79) sts evenly up right front to beg of neck shaping, 62(64:67:69) sts to shoulder, 36(38:40:42) sts across back neck, 62(64:67:69) sts down left front neck and 71(74:76:79) sts to cast-on edge. *302(314:326:338) sts.*

Row 1 P2, [k2, p2] to end.

Row 2 K2, [p2, k2] to end.
Rep the last 2 rows twice more and the first row again.
Buttonhole row Rib 4, work 2 tog, yo [rib 10, work 2 tog, yo] five times, rib to end.
Work a further 8 rows.
Bind off in rib.

ARMBANDS

With right side facing, using size 3 (3.25mm) needles, pick up and k102(106:110:114) sts between markers.
Working in k2, p2 rib as given for frontband, work as foll:
Next 2 rows Rib to last 30 sts, turn.
Next 2 rows Rib to last 24 sts, turn.
Next 2 rows Rib to last 18 sts, turn.
Next 2 rows Rib to last 12 sts, turn.
Next 2 rows Rib to last 6 sts, turn.
Next row Rib to end.
Bind off in rib.

FINISHING

Join side seams. Sew on buttons.

mittens

FINISHED SIZE
To fit small to medium (medium to large) hands.
Length 12(12¼)in/30.5(31)cm.

YARN
3 x 1¾oz/123yd balls of Rowan *Wool Cotton*
Misty 903

NEEDLES
Pair each of size 3 (3.25mm) and size 5 (3.75mm)
knitting needles
Cable needle

GAUGE
29 sts and 32 rows to 4in/10cm square over patt
using size 5 (3.75mm) needles *or size to obtain correct
gauge*.

ABBREVIATIONS
Cr2R—cross 2 right, slip next st on a cable needle and
leave at back of work, k1, then p1 from cable needle.
Cr2L—cross 2 left, slip next st on a cable needle and
leave at front of work, p1, then k1 from cable needle.
Cr2Rtbl—cross 2 right, slip next st on a cable needle
and leave at back of work, k1tbl, then k1tbl from cable
needle.
Cr2Ltbl—cross 2 left, slip next st on a cable needle
and leave at front of work, k1tbl, then k1tbl from cable
needle.
Cr4R—cross 4 right, slip next st on a cable needle and
leave at back of work, k3, then p1 from cable needle.
Cr4L—cross 4 left, slip next 3 sts on a cable needle
and leave at front of work, p1, then k3 from cable
needle.
C7B—cable 7 back, slip next 4 sts on a cable needle
and leave at back of work, k3, slip last st on cable
needle back onto left-hand needle, p this st then k3
from cable needle.
MB—make bobble, [k1, p1, k1, p1, k1] all in next st,

turn, p5, turn, k5, turn, p2tog, p1, p2tog, turn, sk2p to
complete the bobble.
MK—make knot, [k1, p1, k1, p1, k1] all in next st,
turn, p5, turn, pass 2nd, 3rd, and 4th sts over the first
st on left-hand needle, then k1tbl to complete the
knot.
See also page 133.

Patt Panel A (worked over 15(17) sts)
Row 1 P4(5), C7B, p4(5).
Row 2 K4(5), p3, k1, p3, k4(5).
Row 3 P3(4), C4R, p1, C4L, p3(4).
Row 4 K3(4), p3, k3, p3, k3(4).
Row 5 P2(3), C4R, p3, C4L, p2(3).
Row 6 K2(3), p3, k5, p3, k2(3).
Row 7 P2(3), k3, p2, MB, p2, k3, p2(3).
Row 8 K2(3), p3, k5, p3, k2(3).
Row 9 P2(3), C4L, p3, C4R, p2(3).
Row 10 K3(4), p3, k3, p3, k3(4).
Row 11 P3(4), C4L, p1, C4R, p3(4).
Row 12 K4(5), p3, k1, p3, k4(5).
These 12 rows form the patt panel A.

Patt Panel B (worked over 14 sts)
Row 1 P5, Cr2Rtbl, k1, p3, Cr2L, MK.
Row 2 K1, p1, k4, p3, k5.
Row 3 P4, Cr2R, k2, p3, MK, Cr2L.
Row 4 P1, k5, p2, k1, p1, k4.
Row 5 P2, MK, Cr2R, p1, k2, p5, MK.
Row 6 K6, p2, k2, p1, k3.
Row 7 P2, Cr2R, MK, p1, k2, p6.
Row 8 K6, p2, k3, p1, k2.
Row 9 MK, Cr2R, p3, k1, Cr2Ltbl, p5.
Row 10 K4, p4, k4, p1, k1.
Row 11 Cr2R, MK, p3, k2, Cr2L, p4.
Row 12 K4, p1, k1, p2, k5, p1.
Row 13 MK, p5, k2, p1, Cr2L, MK, p2.
Row 14 K3, p1, k2, p2, k6.
Row 15 P6, k2, p1, MK, Cr2L, p2.

Row 16 K2, p1, k3, p2, k6.
These 16 rows form the patt panel.

RIGHT MITT

Using size 3 (3.25mm) needles, cast on 66(72) sts.
Rib 1 (rs) [K1, p1] to end.
This row forms the rib.
Work a further 9 rows, inc one st at center of last row.
67(73) sts.
Change to size 5 (3.75mm) needles and patt.
Row 1 Work 1st row of Patt Panel A, Patt Panel B, [p4, Patt Panel A] twice.
Row 2 [Work 2nd row of Patt Panel A, k4] twice, Patt Panel B, Patt Panel A.
These 2 rows set the position for the patt panels.
Working correct patt rows cont as foll:
Work a further 8 rows.
Dec row Work Patt Panel A, Patt Panel B, [p1, p2tog, p1, Patt Panel A] twice.
Work 7 rows.
Dec row Work Patt Panel A, Patt Panel B, [p2tog, p1, Patt Panel A] twice.
Work 7 rows.
Dec row Work Patt Panel A, Patt Panel B, [p2tog, Patt Panel A] twice.
Work 7 rows.
Dec row Work Patt Panel A, Patt Panel B, [p next st tog with first st of Patt Panel A, work rem 14(16) sts of patt panel A] twice. *59(65) sts.*
Cont in patt as set until mitt measures 6¼in/16cm from cast-on edge, ending with a wrong side row.
Change to size 3 (3.25mm) needles.
Cont in patt as set until mitt measures 8in/20cm from cast-on edge, ending with a wrong side row.
Change to size 5 (3.75mm) needles.
Work a further 4 rows.
Shape thumb
Row 1 Patt 29(31), M1pw, patt 30(34).
Row 2 Patt 30(34), k1, patt 29(31).
Row 3 Patt 29(31), M1pw, p1, M1pw, patt 30(34).
Row 4 Patt 30(34), k3, patt 29(31).
Row 5 Patt 29(31), M1pw, p3, M1pw, patt 30(34).

Row 6 Patt 30(34), k3, patt 29(31).

Cont in this way keeping thumb sts in rev St st and inc 2 sts on every right side row until there are 72(80) sts. Work 1 row.

Divide for thumb

Next row Patt 42(46), turn.

Next row Cast on 1 st, k13(15) sts, turn. *14(16) sts.*

Work 2 rows rev St st.

Next row [K1, p1] to end.

Rep the last row 3 times more.

Bind off in rib.

Join seam.

With RS facing, rejoin yarn to base of thumb, patt to end. *59(65) sts.*

Patt 11 rows, dec 1 st at center. *58(64) sts.*

Rib 1 (rs) [K1, p1] to end.

This row forms the rib.

Work a further 9 rows.

Bind off in rib. Join seam.

LEFT MITT

Using size 3 (3.25mm) needles, cast on 66(72) sts.

Rib 1 (rs) [K1, p1] to end.

This row forms the rib.

Work a further 9 rows, inc one st at center of last row. *67(73) sts.*

Change to size 5 (3.75mm) needles and patt.

Row 1 [Work 1st row of Patt Panel A, p4] twice, Patt Panel B, Patt Panel A.

Row 2 Work 2nd row of Patt Panel A, Patt Panel B, [k4, Patt Panel A] twice.

These 2 rows set the position for the patt panels.

Working correct patt rows cont as foll:

Work a further 8 rows.

Dec row [Work Patt Panel A, p1, p2tog, p1] twice, Patt Panel B, Patt Panel A.

Work 7 rows.

Dec row [Work Patt Panel A, p2tog, p1] twice, Patt Panel B, Patt Panel A.

Work 7 rows.

Dec row [Work Panel A, p2tog] twice, Patt Panel B, Patt Panel A.

Work 7 rows.

Dec row [Work 14(16) sts of Patt Panel A, p last st tog with next st] twice, Patt Panel B, Patt Panel A. *59(65) sts.*

Cont in patt as set until mitt measures 6¼in/16cm from cast-on edge, ending with a wrong side row.

Change to size 3 (3.25mm) needles.

Cont in patt as set until mitt measures 8in/20cm from cast-on edge, ending with a wrong side row.

Change to size 5 (3.75mm) needles.

Work a further 4 rows.

Shape thumb

Row 1 Patt 30(34), M1pw, patt 29(31).

Row 2 Patt 29(31), k1, patt 30(34).

Row 3 Patt 30(34), M1pw, p1, M1pw, patt 29(31).

Row 4 Patt 29(31), k3, patt 30(34).

Row 5 Patt 30(34), M1pw, p3, M1pw, patt 29(31).

Row 6 Patt 29(31), k3, patt 30(34).

Cont in this way keeping thumb sts in rev St st and inc 2 sts on every right side row until there are 72(80) sts. Work 1 row.

Divide for thumb

Next row Patt 43(49), turn.

Next row Cast on 1 st, k13(15) sts, turn. *14(16) sts.*

Work 2 rows rev St st.

Next row [K1, p1] to end.

Rep the last row 3 times more.

Bind off in rib.

Join seam.

With RS facing, rejoin yarn to base of thumb, patt to end. *59(65) sts.*

Patt 11 rows, dec 1 st at center. *58(64) sts.*

Rib 1 (rs) [K1, p1] to end.

This row forms the rib.

Work a further 9 rows.

Bind off in rib.

Join seam.

beret

FINISHED SIZE
To fit an average size head.

YARN
2 x 1¾oz/123yd balls of Rowan *Wool Cotton*
Smalt 963

NEEDLES
Pair each of size 3 (3.25mm) and size 5 (3.75mm)
knitting needles
Circular size 5 (3.75mm) needle
Cable needle

GAUGE
23 sts and 32 rows to 4in/10cm square over St st
using size 5 (3.75mm) needles *or size to obtain correct
gauge.*
29 sts and 32 rows to 4in/10cm square over cable patt
using size 5 (3.75mm) needles *or size to obtain correct
gauge.*

ABBREVIATIONS
Cr2R—cross 2 right, slip next st on a cable needle and
leave at back of work, k1, then p1 from cable needle.
Cr2L—cross 2 left, slip next st on a cable needle and
leave at front of work, p1, then k1 from cable needle.
Cr2Rtbl—cross 2 right, slip next st on a cable needle
and leave at back of work, k1tbl, then k1tbl from cable
needle.
Cr2Ltbl—cross 2 left, slip next st on a cable needle
and leave at front of work, k1tbl, then k1tbl from cable
needle.
Cr4R—cross 4 right, slip next st on a cable needle and
leave at back of work, k3, then p1 from cable needle.
Cr4L—cross 4 left, slip next 3 sts on a cable needle
and leave at front of work, p1, then k3 from cable
needle.
C7B—cable 7 back, slip next 4 sts on a cable needle
and leave at back of work, k3, slip last st on cable

needle back onto left-hand needle, p this st then k3
from cable needle.
MB—make bobble, [k1, p1, k1, p1, k1] all in next st,
turn, p5, turn, k5, turn, p2tog, p1, p2tog, turn, sk2p to
complete the bobble.
MK—make knot, [k1, p1, k1, p1, k1] all in next st,
turn, p5, turn, pass 2nd, 3rd, and 4th sts over the first
st on left-hand needle, then k1tbl to complete the
knot.
See also page 133.

Patt Panel A (worked over 15 sts)
Row 1 P4, C7B, p4.
Row 2 K4, p3, k1, p3, k4.
Row 3 P3, C4R, p1, C4L, p3.
Row 4 K3, p3, k3, p3, k3.
Row 5 P2, C4R, p3, C4L, p2.
Row 6 K2, p3, k5, p3, k2.
Row 7 P2, k3, p2, MB, p2, k3, p2.
Row 8 K2, p3, k5, p3, k2.
Row 9 P2, C4L, p3, C4R, p2.
Row 10 K3, p3, k3, p3, k3.
Row 11 P3, C4L, p1, C4R, p3.
Row 12 K4, p3, k1, p3, k4.
These 12 rows form the Patt Panel A.

Patt Panel B (worked over 14 sts)
Row 1 P5, Cr2Rtbl, k1, p3, Cr2L, MK.
Row 2 K1, p1, k4, p3, k5.
Row 3 P4, Cr2R, k2, p3, MK, Cr2L.
Row 4 P1, k5, p2, k1, p1, k4.
Row 5 P2, MK, Cr2R, p1, k2, p5, MK.
Row 6 K6, p2, k2, p1, k3.
Row 7 P2, Cr2R, MK, p1, k2, p6.
Row 8 K6, p2, k3, p1, k2.
Row 9 MK, Cr2R, p3, k1, Cr2Ltbl, p5.
Row 10 K4, p4, k4, p1, k1.
Row 11 Cr2R, MK, p3, k2, Cr2L, p4.
Row 12 K4, p1, k1, p2, k5, p1.

Row 13 MK, p5, k2, p1, Cr2L, MK, p2.
Row 14 K3, p1, k2, p2, k6.
Row 15 P6, k2, p1, MK, Cr2L, p2.
Row 16 K2, p1, k3, p2, k6.
These 16 rows form the Patt Panel B.

BERET

Using size 3 (3.25mm) needles, cast on 90 sts.
Rib row [K1, p1] to end.
This row forms the rib.
Work a further 10 rows.
Change to size 5 (3.75mm) circular needle.

Work backward and forward in patt.
Inc row P1, [M1, p1] to end. *179 sts.*
Row 1 P3, work across 1st row Patt Panel A, p5, * work across 1st row Patt Panel B, p5, [work across 1st row Patt Panel A, p5] twice; rep from * once more, work across 1st row Patt Panel B, p5, work across 1st row Patt Panel A, p4.
Row 2 K4, work across 2nd row Patt Panel A, k5, * work across 2nd row Patt Panel B, k5, [work across 2nd row Patt Panel A, k5] twice; rep from * once more, work across 2nd row Patt Panel B, k5, work across 2nd row Patt Panel A, k3.

These 2 rows set the patt.

Work a further 36 rows, ending with row 6 of Panel B.

Dec row 1 P3, patt 15, p1, p2tog, p2, * patt 14, p1, p2tog, p2, [patt 15, p1, p2tog, p2] twice; rep from * once more, patt 14, p1, p2tog, p2, patt 15, p1, p2tog, p1. *170 sts.*

Patt 1 row.

Dec row 2 P3, patt 15, p1, p2tog, p1, * patt 14, p1, p2tog, p1, [patt 15, p1, p2tog, p1] twice; rep from * once more, patt 14, p1, p2tog, p1, patt 15, p2tog, p1. *161 sts.*

Patt 1 row.

Dec row 3 P1, p2tog, patt 15, p2tog, p1, * patt 14, p2tog, p1, [patt 15, p2tog, p1] twice; rep from * once more, patt 14, p2tog, p1, patt 15, p2. *152 sts.*

Patt 1 row.

Dec row 4 P2tog, patt 15, p2tog, * patt 14, p2tog, [patt 15, p2tog] twice; rep from * once more, patt 14, p2tog, patt 15, p2. *143 sts.*

Patt 1 row.

Dec row 5 P1, patt 15, p1, * patt 5, k2tog, skp, patt 5, p1, [patt 15, p1] twice; rep from * once more, patt 5, k2tog, skp, patt 5, p1, patt 15, p2. *137 sts.*

Patt 1 row.

Now keep sts to right of central "k2" on Panel B in rev St st cont to dec as foll:

Dec row 6 P1, patt 15, p1, * p4, k2tog, skp, patt 4, p1, [patt 15, p1] twice; rep from * once more, p4, k2tog, skp, patt 4, p1, patt 15, p2. *131 sts.*

Patt 1 row.

Dec row 7 P1, patt 15, p1, * p3, k2tog, skp, patt 3, p1, [patt 15, p1] twice; rep from * once more, p3, k2tog, skp, patt 3, p1, patt 15, p2. *125 sts.*

Patt 1 row.

Dec row 8 P1, patt 15, p1, * p2, k2tog, skp, patt 2, p1, [patt 15, p1] twice; rep from * once more, p2, k2tog, skp, patt 2, p1, patt 15, p2. *119 sts.*

Patt 1 row.

Dec row 9 P1, patt 15, p1, * p1, k2tog, skp, p2, [patt 15, p1] twice; rep from * once more, p1, k2tog, skp, p2, patt 15, p2. *113 sts.*

Patt 1 row.

Dec row 10 P1, patt 15, p1, * k2tog, skp, p1, [patt 15, p1] twice; rep from * once more, k2tog, skp, p1, patt 15, p2. *107 sts.*

Patt 1 row.

Dec row 11 P1, p2tog, patt 13, * k2tog, skp, patt 15, p2tog, patt 14, rep from * once more, k2tog, skp, patt 14, p2tog, p1. *97 sts.*

Patt 1 row.

Dec row 12 P1, p2tog, p1, slip next 3 sts on a cable needle and leave at back of work, p1, [k next st tog with next st on cable needle] 3 times, p3,* k2tog, skp, p3, slip next 3 sts on a cable needle and leave at back of work, p1, [k next st tog with next st on cable needle] 3 times, p8, slip next 3 sts on a cable needle and leave at back of work, p1, [k next st tog with next st on cable needle] 3 times, p3, rep from * once more, k2tog, skp, p3, slip next 3 sts on a cable needle and leave at back of work, p1, [k next st tog with next st on cable needle] 3 times, p2, p2tog, p1. *71 sts.*

Now cont in rev St st.

Next row K to end.

Dec row 13 P3, * [k2tog] twice, p2, k2tog, skp, p2, [k2tog] twice, [p1, p2tog] twice, p2, rep from * once, [k2tog] twice, p2, k2tog, skp, p2, [k2tog] twice, p1, p2tog, p1. *48 sts.*

Next row K to end.

Dec row 14 P2, [p2tog] 22 times p2. *26 sts.*

Next row K to end.

Dec row 15 P1, [p2tog] 12 times, p1. *14 sts.*

Next row K to end.

Dec row 16 P1, [p2tog] 6 times, p1. *8 sts.*

Next row K to end.

Break off yarn, thread through rem sts, and fasten off.

Join seam.

SOCKS

FINISHED SIZE
To fit US shoe size 6–7 (8–9).

YARN
6 x 1¾oz/123yd balls of Rowan *Wool Cotton*
Misty 903

NEEDLES
Pair each of size 3 (3.25mm) and size 5 (3.75mm)
knitting needles
Set of size 5 (3.75mm) double-pointed knitting needles
Cable needle

GAUGE
29 sts and 32 rows to 4in/10cm square over patt
using size 5 (3.75mm) needles *or size to obtain correct
gauge*.

ABBREVIATIONS
Cr2R—cross 2 right, slip next st on a cable needle and
leave at back of work, k1, then p1 from cable needle.
Cr2L—cross 2 left, slip next st on a cable needle and
leave at front of work, p1, then k1 from cable needle.
Cr2Rtbl—cross 2 right, slip next st on a cable needle
and leave at back of work, k1tbl, then k1tbl from cable
needle.
Cr2Ltbl—cross 2 left, slip next st on a cable needle
and leave at front of work, k1tbl, then k1tbl from cable
needle.
Cr4R—cross 4 right, slip next st on a cable needle and
leave at back of work, k3, then p1 from cable needle.
Cr4L—cross 4 left, slip next 3 sts on a cable needle
and leave at front of work, p1, then k3 from cable
needle.
C7B—cable 7 back, slip next 4 sts on a cable needle
and leave at back of work, k3, slip last st on cable
needle back onto left-hand needle, p this st then k3
from cable needle.
MB—make bobble, [k1, p1, k1, p1, k1] all in next st,
turn, p5, turn, k5, turn, p2tog, p1, p2tog, turn, sk2p to
complete the bobble.
MK—make knot, [k1, p1, k1, p1, k1] all in next st,
turn, p5, turn, pass 2nd, 3rd, and 4th sts over the first
st on left-hand needle, then k1tbl to complete the
knot.
Wrap 1—with yarn to front, slip next st, turn, bring
yarn to front, slip st back onto right-hand needle.
See also page 133.

Patt Panel A (worked over 15 sts)
Row 1 P4, C7B, p4.
Row 2 K4, p3, k1, p3, k4.
Row 3 P3, C4R, p1, C4L, p3.
Row 4 K3, p3, k3, p3, k3.
Row 5 P2, C4R, p3, C4L, p2.
Row 6 K2, p3, k5, p3, k2.
Row 7 P2, k3, p2, MB, p2, k3, p2.
Row 8 K2, p3, k5, p3, k2.
Row 9 P2, C4L, p3, C4R, p2.
Row 10 K3, p3, k3, p3, k3.
Row 11 P3, C4L, p1, C4R, p3.
Row 12 K4, p3, k1, p3, k4.
These 12 rows form the Patt Panel A.

Patt Panel B (worked over 14 sts)
Row 1 P5, Cr2Rtbl, k1, p3, Cr2L, MK.
Row 2 K1, p1, k4, p3, k5.
Row 3 P4, Cr2R, k2, p3, MK, Cr2L.
Row 4 P1, k5, p2, k1, p1, k4.
Row 5 P2, MK, Cr2R, p1, k2, p5, MK.
Row 6 K6, p2, k2, p1, k3.
Row 7 P2, Cr2R, MK, p1, k2, p6.
Row 8 K6, p2, k3, p1, k2.
Row 9 MK, Cr2R, p3, k1, Cr2Ltbl, p5.
Row 10 K4, p4, k4, p1, k1.
Row 11 Cr2R, MK, p3, k2, Cr2L, p4.
Row 12 K4, p1, k1, p2, k5, p1.
Row 13 MK, p5, k2, p1, Cr2L, MK, p2.

Row 14 K3, p1, k2, p2, k6.

Row 15 P6, k2, p1, MK, Cr2L, p2.

Row 16 K2, p1, k3, p2, k6.

These 16 rows form the Patt Panel B.

SOCK (make 2)

Using size 3 (3.25mm) needles, cast on 92 sts.

Row 1 (rs) [K1, p1] to end.

This row forms the rib.

Work a further 9 rows.

Change to size 5 (3.75mm) needles and patt.

Row 1 P2, [work 1st row of Patt Panel A, Patt Panel B, Patt Panel A] twice, p2.

Row 2 K2, [work 2nd row of Patt Panel A, Patt Panel B, Patt Panel A] twice, k2.

These 2 rows set the position for the patt panels.

Work a further 106 rows, ending with row 12 of Panel A and row 12 of Panel B.

Dec row P2, * [p2tog] twice, slip next 4 sts on a cable needle and leave at back of work, [k next st tog with first st on cable needle] 3 times, then p1 cable needle, [p2tog] 5 times, k2tog, p1, k2tog, p1, [p2tog] 3 times, slip next 4 sts on a cable needle and leave at back of work, [k next st tog with first st on cable needle] 3 times, then p1 cable needle, [p2tog] twice; rep from * once more, p2. *52 sts.*

Next row P25, p2tog, p25. *51 sts.*

Cut yarn.

Cont on double-pointed needles and St st.

Shape heel

Slip next 13 sts on first needle, next 13 sts on second needle, next 13 sts on third needle and last 12 sts on end of first needle.

Rejoin yarn to beg of first needle.

Next row K24, wrap 1.

Next row P23, wrap 1.

Next row K22, wrap 1.

Next row P21, wrap 1.

Cont in this way, working one less st on every row until the foll row has been worked:

Next row P11, wrap 1.

Next row K11, wrap 1.

Next row P12, wrap 1.

Cont in this way, working one more st on every row until the foll row has been worked:

Next row K23, wrap 1.

Next row P24, wrap first st on next needle

With right side facing, slip next 17 sts on first needle, next 17 sts on second needle and next 17 sts on third needle.

Cont in rounds of St st until sock measures 5½(6)in/ 14(15)cm from last dec row, decreasing one st at end of last round.

Shape toe

Next round [K1, skp, k19, k2tog, k1] twice.

Next round K to end.

Next round [K1, skp, k17, k2tog, k1] twice.

Next round K to end.

Next round [K1, skp, k15, k2tog, k1] twice.

Next round K to end.

Cont in rounds decreasing on every alt round as set until the foll round has been worked.

Next round [K1, skp, k7, k2tog, k1] twice.

Slip first 11 sts onto one needle and rem 11 sts onto a second needle.

Fold sock inside out and cast one st from each needle off together.

adair

This elegant shrug is knitted in Rowan *Cashsoft 4 ply*, which shows up the cable detail beautifully while remaining exquisitely soft. The pattern is a 12-stitch unusual three-strand cable, separated by stockinette stitch panels. The construction looks complicated but is, in fact, surprisingly simple. The back piece is knitted first, and then the long cable border, the cast-on/bound-off edges of which are joined together at the back of the neck, before the border is joined to the back piece. The front part of the border creates a gently rolling neckline for the shrug and a deep, horizontal band for the back.

MEASUREMENTS

To fit bust

S	M	L	XL	
32–34	36–38	40–42	44–46	in
82–87	92–97	102–107	112–117	cm

Actual measurements

Across back

18	20½	22½	25	in
46	52	57	63	cm

Length to shoulder

17¾	18	18½	19	in
45	46	47	48	cm

YARN

6(6:7:7) x 1¾oz/197yd balls of Rowan *Cashsoft 4 ply* Weather 425

NEEDLES

Pair of size 3 (3.25mm) knitting needles
Circular size 3 (3.25mm) knitting needle
Cable needle

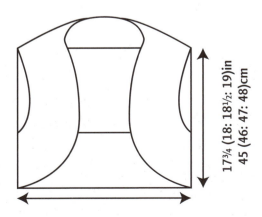

17¾ (18: 18½: 19)in
45 (46: 47: 48)cm

GAUGE

28 sts and 36 rows to 4in/10cm square over St st using size 3 (3.25mm) needles *or size to obtain correct gauge.*

36 sts and 36 rows to 4in/10cm square over cable patt (stretched) using size 3 (3.25mm) needles *or size to obtain correct gauge.*

ABBREVIATIONS

Cr12fb—slip next 8 sts on a cable needle and leave at front of work, k4, then slip the last 4 sts—to the left of cable needle—back onto left-hand needle, take the cable needle to the back of work, k4 from left-hand needle, then k4 from cable needle.

Cr12bf—slip next 8 sts on a cable needle and leave at back of work, k4, then slip the last 4 sts—to the left of cable needle—back onto left-hand needle, bring the cable needle to the front of work, k4 from left-hand needle, then k4 from cable needle.

See also page 133.

BACK

Using size 3 (3.25mm) circular needle, cast on 168(184:200:216) sts.
Work backward and forward in rows.
Row 1 (rs) P2, k4, p2, [k8, p2, k4, p2] to end.
Row 2 K2, p4, k2, [p8, k2, p4, k2] to end.
Row 3 (inc row) P2, k4, p2, * k1, M1, [k2, M1] 3 times, k1, p2, k4, p2; rep from * to end.
208(228:248:268) sts.
Row 4 K2, p4, k2, [p12, k2, p4, k2] to end.
Cont in patt.
Row 1 (rs) P2, k4, p2, [Cr12fb, p2, k4, p2] to end.
Row 2 K2, p4, k2, [p12, k2, p4, k2] to end.
Row 3 P2, k4, p2, [k12, p2, k4, p2] to end.
Row 4 K2, p4, k2, [p12, k2, p4, k2] to end.
Rows 5 to 10 Rep rows 3 and 4 three times more.
Row 11 P2, k4, p2, [Cr12bf, p2, k4, p2] to end.
Row 12 K2, p4, k2, [p12, k2, p4, k2] to end.
Rows 13 to 18 Rep rows 3 and 4 three times more.
Row 19 P2, k4, p2, [k1, k2tog] 4 times, p2, k4, p2, [k12, p2, k4, p2] to last 20 sts, [k1, k2tog] 4 times,

p2, k4, p2.

Row 20 Bind off 16 sts knit wise, patt to last 16 sts, bind off these 16 sts knitwise. *168(188:208:228) sts.* Break off yarn.

These 20 rows form the cable panel.

With right side facing, rejoin yarn to rem sts.

Now cont in cable panel as set.

Work even for a further 75(79:83:87) rows.

Next row P6, * k2, [p1, p2tog] 4 times, k2, p4; rep from * to last 2 sts, p2. *136(152:168:184) sts.* Bind off.

BORDER

Using size 3 (3.25mm) needles, cast on 56 sts.

Row 1 (rs) P2, k4, p2, [k8, p2, k4, p2] to end.

Row 2 K2, p4, k2, [p8, k2, p4, k2] to end.

Row 3 (inc row) P2, k4, p2, * k1, M1, [k2, M1] 3 times, k1, p2, k4, p2; rep from * to end. *68 sts.*

Row 4 K2, p4, k2, [p12, k2, p4, k2] to end.

Cont in patt.

Row 1 (rs) P2, k4, p2, [Cr12fb, p2, k4, p2] to end.

Row 2 P6, k2, [p12, k2, p4, k2] to end.

Row 3 P2, k4, p2, [k12, p2, k4, p2] to end.

Row 4 P6, k2, [p12, k2, p4, k2] to end.

Rows 5 to 10 Rep rows 3 and 4 three times more.

Row 11 P2, k4, p2, [Cr12bf, p2, k4, p2] to end.

Row 12 P6, k2, [p12, k2, p4, k2] to end.

Rows 13 to 20 Rep rows 3 and 4 four times more.

These 20 rows form the patt.

Work a further 84(92:100:108) rows.

Mark end of last row with a colored thread.

Now cont in cable panel as set.

Work a further 76(80:84:88) rows.

Mark end of last row with a colored thread.

Work a further 136(152:168:184) rows.

Mark end of last row with a colored thread.

Work a further 76(80:84:88) rows.

Mark end of last row with a colored thread.

Work a further 105(113:121:129) rows.

Next row P6, * k2, [p1, p2tog] 4 times, k2, p4; rep from * to last 2 sts, k2. *56 sts.*

Next row P2, k4, p2, [k8, p2, k4, p2] to end.

Next row P4, k2, [p8, k2, p4, k2] to end.

Bind off.

FINISHING

Join cast-on and bound-off edges of border. With border seam to center of cast-on edge of back, sew border around outside edge of back, match first colored thread to left armhole, second colored thread to left shoulder, third colored thread to right shoulder, fourth colored thread to right armhole.

Lara

This is an updated version of a classic cardigan, with a more boxy shape. The cables provide lovely finishing touches, with a horizontal band of braided cable on the upper sleeve and neat fine cable detail on the cuffs and welt, as well as on the pocket tops and button bands. Knitted in gently flecked Rowan *Felted Tweed DK*, it can be dressed up or down to suit the occasion.

MEASUREMENTS

To fit bust

S	M	L	XL	
32–34	36–38	40–42	44–46	in
82–87	92–97	102–107	112–117	cm

Actual measurements

Bust

48½	54	59½	65	in
123	137	151	165	cm

Length to shoulder

20	21	21¾	22½	in
51	53	55	57	cm

Sleeve length

17in/43cm

YARN

8(9:9:10) x 1¾oz/191yd balls of Rowan *Felted Tweed DK* Duck Egg 173

NEEDLES

Pair each of size 2/3 (3mm) and size 5 (3.75mm) knitting needles
Circular size 5 (3.75mm) needle
Cable needle

EXTRAS

Six buttons (½in/15mm diameter)

GAUGE

23 sts and 32 rows to 4in/10cm over St st using size 5 (3.75mm) needles *or size to obtain correct gauge.*

ABBREVIATIONS

C4B—cable 4 back, slip next 2 sts on cable needle and hold at back of work, k2 then k2 from cable needle.
C12B—cable 12 back, slip next 6 sts on cable needle and hold at back of work, k6 then k6 from cable needle.
C12F—cable 12 front, slip next 6 sts on cable needle and hold at front of work, k6 then k6 from cable needle.
See also page 133.

BACK

Using size 2/3 (3mm) needles, cast on 176(196:216:236) sts.
Row 1 (rs) P2, k2, p2, [k4, p2, k2, p2] to end.
Row 2 K2, p2, k2, [p4, k2, p2, k2] to end.
Row 3 P2, k2, p2, [C4B, p2, k2, p2] to end.

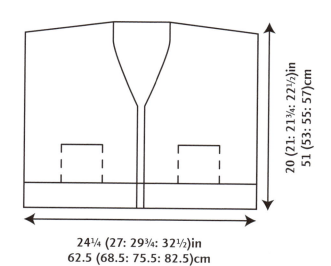

24¼ (27: 29¾: 32½)in
62.5 (68.5: 75.5: 82.5)cm

20 (21: 21¾: 22½)in
51 (53: 55: 57)cm

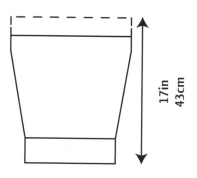

17in
43cm

Row 4 As row 2.

Rows 5 to 22 Rep rows 1 to 4 four times more and rows 1 and 2 again.

Row 23 [P2, k2, p2, * slip next 2 sts on cable needle and hold at back of work, k next st tog with first st on cable needle] twice, p2, k2, p2; rep from * to end. *142(158:174:190)sts.*

Row 24 K2, [p2, k2] to end.

Change to size 5 (3.75mm) needles.

Beg with a k row cont in St st until back measures 19(19¾:20½¼:21¼)in/48(50:52:54)cm from cast-on edge, ending with a wrong side row.

Shape upper arms

Bind off 7(8:9:10) sts at beg of next 8 rows and 9 sts at beg of foll 2 rows.

Shape shoulders

Bind off 8(9:10:11) sts at beg of next 4 rows.

Leave rem 36(40:44:48) sts on a spare needle.

POCKET LININGS (make 2)

Using size 5 (3.75mm) needles, cast on 34(34:36:36) sts.

Beg with a k row work 25(27:29:31) rows in St st.

Leave these sts on a holder.

LEFT FRONT

Using size 2/3 (3mm) needles, cast on 86(96:106:116) sts.

Row 1 (rs) P2, k2, p2, [k4, p2, k2, p2] to end.

Row 2 K2, p2, k2, [p4, k2, p2, k2] to end.

Row 3 P2, k2, p2, [C4B, p2, k2, p2] to end.

Row 4 As row 2.

Rows 5 to 22 Rep rows 1 to 4 four times more and rows 1 and 2 again.

Row 23 [P2, k2, p2, * slip next 2 sts on cable needle and hold at back of work, k next st tog with first st on cable needle] twice, p2, k2, p2; rep from * to end. *70(78:86:94) sts.*

Row 24 K2, [p2, k2] to end.

Change to size 5 (3.75mm) needles.

Beg with a k row work 24(26:28:30) rows in St st.

Place pocket lining

Next row K to last 45(48:50:53) sts, bind off 34(34:36:36) sts, k to end.

Next row P11(14:14:17), p across 34(34:36:36) sts of pocket lining, p to end.

Cont in St st until front measures 11(11½:11¾:12¼) in/28(29:30:31)cm from cast-on edge, ending with a wrong side row.

Shape front neck

Next row K to last 4 sts, k2tog, k2.

Next row P to end.

Rep the last 2 rows 5(7:9:11) times.

Next row K to last 4 sts, k2tog, k2.

Work 3 rows.

Rep the last 4 rows until 53(59:65:71) sts rem.

Work even until front measures the same as back to upper arm shaping, ending at side edge.

Shape upper arm

Bind off 7(8:9:10) sts at beg of next and 3 foll right side rows.

Work 1 row.

Bind off 9 sts at beg of next row.

Work 1 row.

Shape shoulder

Bind off 8(9:10:11) sts at beg of next row.

Work 1 row.

Bind off rem 8(9:10:11) sts.

RIGHT FRONT

Using size 2/3 (3mm) needles, cast on 86(96:106:116) sts.

Row 1 (rs) P2, k2, p2, [k4, p2, k2, p2] to end.

Row 2 K2, p2, k2, [p4, k2, p2, k2] to end.

Row 3 P2, k2, p2, [C4B, p2, k2, p2] to end.

Row 4 As row 2.

Rows 5 to 22 Rep rows 1 to 4 four times more and rows 1 and 2 again.

Row 23 [P2, k2, p2, * slip next 2 sts on cable needle and hold at back of work, k next st tog with firSt st on cable needle] twice, p2, k2, p2; rep from * to end. *70(78:86:94) sts.*

Row 24 K2, [p2, k2] to end.

Change to size 5 (3.75mm) needles.

Beg with a k row work 24(26:28:30) rows in St st.

Place pocket lining

Next row K11(14:14:17), bind off 34(34:36:36) sts, k to end.

Next row P to last 11(14:14:17) sts, p across 34(34:36:36) sts of pocket lining, p to end.

Cont in St st until front measures 11(11½:11¾: 12¼)in/28(29:30:31)cm from cast-on edge, ending with a wrong side row.

Shape front neck

Next row K2, skp, k to end.

Next row P to end.

Rep the last 2 rows 5(7:9:11) times.

Next row K2, skp, k to end.

Work 3 rows.

Rep the last 4 rows until 53(59:65:71) sts rem.

Work even until front measures the same as back to upper arm shaping, ending at side edge.

Shape upper arm

Bind off 7(8:9:10) sts at beg of next and 3 foll wrong side rows.

Work 1 row.

Bind off 9 sts at beg of next row.

Work 1 row.

Shape shoulder

Bind off 8(9:10:11) sts at beg of next row.

Work 1 row.

Bind off rem 8(9:10:11) sts.

SLEEVES

Using size 2/3 (3mm) needles, cast on 66(66:76:76) sts.

Row 1 (rs) P2, k2, p2, [k4, p2, k2, p2] to end.

Row 2 K2, p2, k2, [p4, k2, p2, k2] to end.

Row 3 P2, k2, p2, [C4B, p2, k2, p2] to end.

Row 4 As row 2.

Rows 5 to 22 Rep rows 1 to 4 four times more and rows 1 and 2 again.

Row 23 P2, k2, p2, * slip next 2 sts on cable needle and hold at back of work, [k next st tog with first st on cable needle] twice, p2, k2, p2; rep from * to end. *54(54:62:62) sts.*

Row 24 P to end, inc 0(4:0:4) sts evenly across row. *54(58:62:66) sts.*

Change to size 5 (3.75mm) needles.

Beg with a k row cont in St st.

Work 4 rows.

Inc row K4, M1, k to last 4 sts, M1, k4.

Work 7 rows.

Rep the last 8 rows 8 times more and the inc row again. *74(78:82:86) sts.*

Work even until sleeve measures 13¾in/35cm from cas-on edge, ending with a p row.

Bind off.

CABLE INSERTS (make 2)

Using size 5 (3.75mm) needles cast on 22 sts.

Row 1 K3, p2, k12, p2, k3.

Row 2 P3, k2, p12, k2, p3.

Rep the last 2 rows 0(1:2:3) times more and row 1 again.

Next row P3, k2, p7, [M1, p1] 5 times, M1, k2, p3. *28 sts.*

Now work in cable patt.

Row 1 K3, p2, k18, p2, k3.

Row 2 P3, k2, p18, k2, p3.

Row 3 K3, p2, C12B, k6, p2, k3.

Row 4 P3, k2, p18, k2, p3.

Rows 5 to 10 Rep rows 1 and 2 three times more.

Row 11 K3, p2, k6, C12F, p2, k3.

Row 12 P3, k2, p18, k2, p3.

Rows 13 to 16 Rep rows 1 and 2 twice more.

These 16 rows form the patt.

Work a further 74 rows, ending row 10.

Row 91 K3, p2, k6, slip next 6 sts on cable needle and hold at front of work, [k next st tog with first st on cable needle] 6 times, p2, k3. *22 sts.*

Row 92 P3, k2, p12, k2, p3.

Row 93 K3, p2, k12, p2, k3.

Rep the last 2 rows 0(1:2:3) times more and row 92 again.

Bind off.

POCKET BORDER

Using size 5 (3.75mm) needles cast on 8 sts.

Row 1 K8.

Row 2 K2, C4B, k2.

Row 3 K8.

Row 4 K2, p4, k2.

These 4 rows form the patt.

Cont in patt until border fits across pocket top.

Bind off.

FRONT BORDER

Join shoulder and upper arm seams.

With right side facing, size 5 (3.75mm) circular needle, pick up and k78(80:82:84) sts up right front to beg of neck shaping, 57(58:59:60) sts to shoulder, k36(40:44:48) sts from back neck, pick up and k57(58:59:60) sts down left front to beg of neck shaping, 78(80:82:84) sts to cast-on edge. *306(316:326:336) sts.*

Row 1 K2, p2, k2, [p4, k2, p2, k2] to end.

Row 2 P2, k2, p2, [k4, p2, k2, p2] to end.

Row 3 K2, p2, k2, [p4, k2, p2, k2] to end.

Row 4 P2, k2, p2, [C4B, p2, k2, p2] to end.

These 4 rows form the patt.

Work 1 row.

Buttonhole row 1 P2, k2tog, y2o, p2tog, [patt 10, work 2 tog, y2o, work 2 tog] 5 times, patt to end.

Buttonhole row 2 Patt to end, working twice into yarn.

Patt 3 rows.

Bind off in rib.

FINISHING

Sew one side of Cable insert across top of sleeve. With center of insert to upper arm seam, sew inset to back and front. Join side and sleeve seams.

Sew down pocket linings. Sew pocket borders to top of pocket openings. Sew on buttons.

skye

This very simple, feminine little shrug in a delicate vintage cable and lace pattern, knitted in Rowan *Cashsoft 4 ply*, drapes beautifully. The stitches are inspired by the exquisite lace textures found on traditional Shetland lace scarves and shawls, and are simple to work and give a lovely "ripple effect" texture. The long front pieces can be tied or crossed over at the front, wrapped around the body, or pinned with a brooch. It looks just right worn over a pretty floral dress.

MEASUREMENTS

	S	M	L	XL	
To fit bust					
	32–34	36–38	40–42	44–46	in
	82–87	92–97	102–107	112–117	cm
Actual measurements					
Bust					
	39½	44	46¾	51¼	in
	100	112	119	130	cm
Length to shoulder					
	10¼	11	12¼	13	in
	26	28	31	33	cm

YARN

5(5:6:6) x 1¾oz/197yd balls of Rowan *Cashsoft 4 ply*
Almond 458

NEEDLES

Pair of size 3 (3.25mm) knitting needles
Cable needle

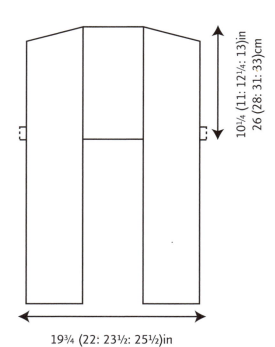

19¾ (22: 23½: 25½)in
50 (56: 59.5: 65)cm

10¼ (11: 12¼: 13)in
26 (28: 31: 33)cm

GAUGE

28 sts and 36 rows to 4in/10cm square over St st
using size 3 (3.25mm) needles *or size to obtain correct
gauge.*
30 sts and 36 rows to 4in/10cm square over lace patt
using size 3 (3.25mm) needles *or size to obtain correct
gauge.*

ABBREVIATIONS

Cr4R—cross 4 right, slip next 2 sts on a cable needle
and leave at back of work, k2, yo, then skp from cable
needle.
See also page 133.

BACK

Using size 3 (3.25mm) needles, cast on
156(176:186:206) sts.
Row 1 (rs) P2, k2tog, yo, p2, [k2, yo, skp, p2, k2tog,
yo, p2] to end.
Row 2 P4, k2, [p2, yo, p2tog, k2, p2, k2] to last 10
sts, p2, yo, p2tog, k2, p4.
Row 3 P2, yo, skp, p2, [k2, yo, skp, p2, yo, skp, p2] to
end.
Row 4 As row 2.
Row 5 P2, k2tog, yo, p2, [Cr4R, p2, k2tog, yo, p2] to
end.
Row 6 As row 2.
Row 7 As row 3.
Row 8 As row 2.
These 8 rows form the patt.
Work a further 4(8:12:16) rows.
Shape armholes
Bind off 10(14:14:20) sts at beg of next 2 rows.
136(148:158:166) sts
Work a further 9(9½:9¾:10¼)in/23(24:25:26)cm,
ending with a wrong side row.
Shape shoulders
Bind off 6 sts at beg of next 12 rows and 10(14:14:17)
sts at beg of foll 2 rows.
Bind off rem 44(48:58:60) sts.

LEFT FRONT

Using size 3 (3.25mm) needles, cast on 46(56:56:66) sts.

Cont in patt as given for back until front measures 17¾in/45cm, ending with a wrong side row.

Mark end of last row with a colored thread.

Work a further 12(16:20:24) rows.

Mark end of last row with a colored thread.

Work a further 9(9½:9¾:10¼)in/23(24:25:26)cm, ending with a wrong side row.

Shape shoulder

Bind off 6(7:7:8) sts at beg of next and 5 foll right side rows.

Work 1 row.

Bind off rem 10(14:14:18) sts.

RIGHT FRONT

Using size 3 (3.25mm) needles, cast on 46(56:56:66) sts.

Cont in patt as given for back until front measures 17¾in/45cm, ending with a wrong side row.

Mark beg of last row with a colored thread.

Work a further 12(16:20:24) rows.

Mark beg of last row with a colored thread.

Work a further 9in/23cm, ending with a right side row.

Shape shoulder

Bind off 6(7:7:8) sts at beg of next and 5 foll wrong side rows.

Work 1 row.

Bind off rem 10(14:14:18) sts.

FINISHING

Join shoulder seams, easing fronts to fit back. Sew rows between markers to first 12(16:20:24) rows of back to form side seams.

kilmory

This is a modern version of a traditional gansey, one of the most popular seed stitch and waving cable Aran designs. It has two different cable designs, worked in pairs. The welt, with its side splits, and the cuffs are finished in garter stitch, while the neckline, which is slightly cut away, is gently ribbed. Knitted in Rowan *Felted Tweed Aran*, it is the ideal sweater to wear with jeans.

MEASUREMENTS

	S	M	L	XL	
To fit bust					
	32–34	36–38	40–42	44–46	in
	82–87	92–97	102–107	112–117	cm
Actual measurements					
Bust					
	41¼	45¼	49¼	53¼	in
	105	115	125	135	cm
Length to shoulder					
	26¾	27½	28¼	29	in
	68	70	72	74	cm
Sleeve length					
	17¾	18	18½	19	in
	45	46	47	48	cm

YARN

14(15:16:17) x 1¾oz/95yd balls of Rowan *Felted Tweed Aran* Storm Blue 730

NEEDLES

Pair each of size 6 (4mm) and size 8 (5mm) knitting needles
Cable needle

GAUGE

16 sts and 23 rows to 4in/10cm square over St st using size 8 (5mm) needles *or size to obtain correct gauge.*

ABBREVIATIONS

C8F — cable 8 front, slip next 4 sts on a cable needle and leave at front of work, k4, then k4 from cable needle.
Cr4R — cross 4 right, slip next st on a cable needle and leave at back of work, k3, then p1 from cable needle.
Cr4L — cross 4 left, slip next 3 sts on a cable needle and leave at front of work, p1, then k3 from cable needle.
See also page 133.

Panel A (worked over 8 sts)
Row 1 K8.
Row 2 P8.
Rows 3 and 4 As rows 1 and 2.
Row 5 C8F.
Row 6 P8.
Rows 7 and 8 As rows 1 and 2.
These 8 rows form the patt and are repeated.

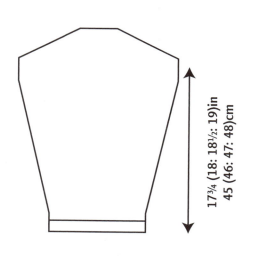

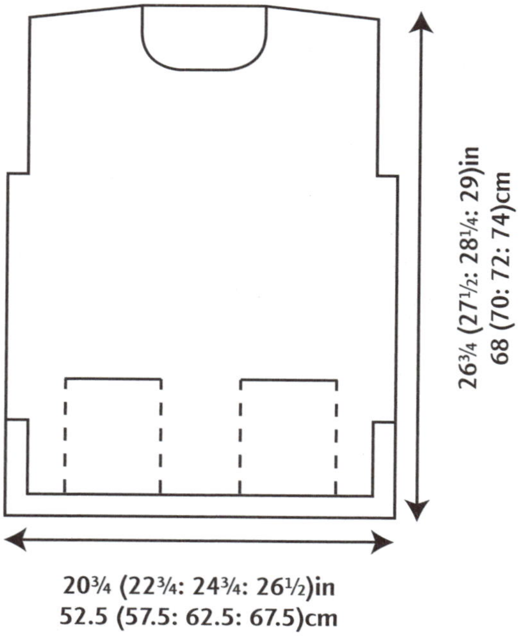

20¾ (22¾: 24¾: 26½)in
52.5 (57.5: 62.5: 67.5)cm

26¾ (27½: 28¼: 29)in
68 (70: 72: 74)cm

17¾ (18: 18½: 19)in
45 (46: 47: 48)cm

Panel B (worked over 11 sts)
Row 1 [P1, k1] 3 times, Cr4R, p1.
Row 2 P1, k1, p3, [k1, p1] 3 times.
Row 3 [P1, k1] twice, p1, Cr4R, k1, p1.
Row 4 P1, k1, p5, [k1, p1] twice.
Row 5 [P1, k1] twice, Cr4R, p1, k1, p1.
Row 6 [P1, k1] twice, p3, [k1, p1] twice.
Row 7 P1, k1, p1, Cr4R, [k1, p1] twice.
Row 8 [P1, k1] twice, p5, k1, p1.
Row 9 P1, k1, Cr4R, p1, [k1, p1] twice.
Row 10 [P1, k1] 3 times, p3, k1, p1.
Row 11 P1, Cr4R, [k1, p1] 3 times.
Row 12 [P1, k1] 3 times, p5.
Row 13 P1, Cr4L, [k1, p1] 3 times.
Row 14 [P1, k1] 3 times, p3, k1, p1.
Row 15 P1, k1, Cr4L, p1, [k1, p1] twice.
Row 16 [P1, k1] twice, p5, k1, p1.
Row 17 P1, k1, p1, Cr4L, [k1, p1] twice.
Row 18 [P1, k1] twice, p3, [k1, p1] twice.
Row 19 [P1, k1] twice, Cr4L, p1, k1, p1.
Row 20 P1, k1, p5, [k1, p1] twice.
Row 21 [P1, k1] twice, p1, Cr4L, k1, p1.
Row 22 P1, k1, p3, [k1, p1] 3 times.
Row 23 [P1, k1] 3 times, Cr4L, p1.

Row 24 P5, [k1, p1] 3 times.
These 24 rows form the patt and are repeated.

Panel C (worked over 11 sts)
Row 1 P1, Cr4L, [k1, p1] 3 times.
Row 2 [P1, k1] 3 times, p3, k1, p1.
Row 3 P1, k1, Cr4L, p1, [k1, p1] twice.
Row 4 [P1, k1] twice, p5, k1, p1.
Row 5 P1, k1, p1, Cr4L, [k1, p1] twice.
Row 6 [P1, k1] twice, p3, [k1, p1] twice.
Row 7 [P1, k1] twice, Cr4L, p1, k1, p1.
Row 8 P1, k1, p5, [k1, p1] twice.
Row 9 [P1, k1] twice, p1, Cr4L, k1, p1.
Row 10 P1, k1, p3, [k1, p1] 3 times.
Row 11 [P1, k1] 3 times, Cr4L, p1.
Row 12 P5, [k1, p1] 3 times.
Row 13 [P1, k1] 3 times, Cr4R, p1.
Row 14 P1, k1, p3, [k1, p1] 3 times.
Row 15 [P1, k1] twice, p1, Cr4R, k1, p1.
Row 16 P1, k1, p5, [k1, p1] twice.
Row 17 [P1, k1] twice, Cr4R, p1, k1, p1.
Row 18 [P1, k1] twice, p3, [k1, p1] twice.
Row 19 P1, k1, p1, Cr4R, [k1, p1] twice.
Row 20 [P1, k1] twice, p5, k1, p1.
Row 21 P1, k1, Cr4R, p1, [k1, p1] twice.
Row 22 [P1, k1] 3 times, p3, k1, p1.
Row 23 P1, Cr4R, [k1, p1] 3 times.
Row 24 [P1, k1] 3 times, p5.
These 24 rows form the patt and are repeated.

BACK
Using size 6 (4mm) needles, cast on 86(94:102:110)
sts.
K 9 rows. Change to size 8 (5mm) needles.
Row 1 K to end.
Row 2 K5, p to last 5 sts, k5.
Rep the last 2 rows 10 times more.
Beg with a k row cont in St st until back measures
13¾in/35cm from cast-on edge, ending with a k row.
Inc row P8(12:16:20), [M1, p2, M1, p15] 4 times, M1,
p2, M1, p8(12:16:20). *96(104:112:120) sts.*
Cont in yoke patt.

Row 1 [K1, p1] 3(5:7:9) times, work across row 1 of patt panels [A, B, A, C] twice, A, [p1, k1] 3(5:7:9) times.

Row 2 [K1, p1] 3(5:7:9) times, work across row 2 of patt panels [A, C, A, B] twice, A, [p1, k1] 3(5:7:9) times.

These 2 rows set the position for patt panels.

Work even until back measures 18½(19:19¼: 19¾)in/47(48:49:50)cm from cast-on edge, ending with a wrong side row.

Shape armholes

Bind off 4(6:8:10) sts at beg of next 2 rows. *88(92:96:100) sts.*

Cont straight until back measures 26¾(27½:28¼:29) in/68(70:72:74)cm from cast-on edge, ending with a wrong side.

Shape shoulders

Bind off 5 sts at beg of next 4 rows, and 10(11:12:13) sts on foll 2 rows.

Leave rem 48(50:52:54) sts on a holder.

POCKET LININGS (make 2)

Using size 8 (5mm) needles, cast on 24(25:26:27) sts.

Beg with a k row work 40 rows in St st.

Leave these sts on a spare needle.

FRONT

Using size 6 (4mm) needles, cast on 86(94:102:110) sts.

K 9 rows. Change to size 8 (5mm) needles.

Row 1 K to end.

Row 2 K5, p to last 5 sts, k5.

Rep the last 2 rows 10 times more.

Beg with a k row work 11 rows in St st.

Next row P10(11:12:13), k24(25:26:27), p18(22:26:30), k24(25:26:27), p10(11:12:13).

Next row K to end.

Rep the last 2 rows twice more.

Next row P10(11:12:13), bind off 24(25:26:27) sts, p next 17(21:25:29) sts, bind off 24(25:26:27) sts, p to end.

Next row K10(11:12:13), k across 24(25:26:27) sts of first pocket lining, k18(22:26:30), k across 24(25:26:27) sts of second pocket lining, k10(11:12:13).

Cont in St st until front measures 13¾in/35cm from cast-on edge, ending with a k row.

Inc row P8(12:16:20), [M1, p2, M1, p15] 4 times, M1, p2, M1, p8(12:16:20). *96(104:112:120) sts.*

Cont in yoke patt.

Row 1 [K1, p1] 3(5:7:9) times, work across row 1 of patt panels [A, B, A, C] twice, A, [p1, k1] 3(5:7:9) times.

Row 2 [K1, p1] 3(5:7:9) times, work across row 2 of patt panels [A, C, A, B] twice, A, [p1, k1] 3(5:7:9) times.

These 2 rows set the position for patt panels.

Work even until front measures 18½(19:19¼:19¾)in/ 47(48:49:50)cm from cast-on edge, ending with a wrong side row.

Shape armholes

Bind off 4(6:8:10) sts at beg of next 2 rows. *88(92:96:100) sts.*

Cont straight until front measures 24(24¾:25¼:26) in/61(63:64:66)cm from cast-on edge, ending with a wrong side row.

Shape neck

Next row Patt 27(28:29:30), turn and work on these sts for first side of neck.

Dec on st at neck edge on the next 4 rows and 3 foll right side rows. *20(21:22:23) sts.*

Work even until front measures the same as back to shoulder, ending at armhole edge.

Shape shoulder

Bind off 5 sts at beg of next and foll right side row.

Work 1 row.

Bind off rem 10(11:12:13) sts.

With right side facing, slip center 34(36:38:40) sts on a holder, rejoin yarn to rem sts, patt to end.

Dec on st at neck edge on the next 4 rows and 3 foll right side rows. *20(21:22:23) sts.*

Work even until front measures the same as back to shoulder, ending at armhole edge.

Shape shoulder

Bind off 5 sts at beg of next and foll wrong side row.

Work 1 row.

Bind off rem 10(11:12:13) sts.

SLEEVES

Using size 6 (4mm) needles, cast on 40(44:48:52) sts.

K 9 rows.

Change to size 8 (5mm) needles.

Beg with a k row cont in St st.

Work 6(4:4:2) rows.

Inc row K3, M1, k to last 3 sts, M1, k3.

Work 5 rows.

Rep the last 6 rows 12 times more and the inc row again. *68(72:76:80) sts.*

Cont even until sleeve measures 17¾(18:18½:19)in/ 45(46:47:48)cm, ending with a p row.

Place markers at each end of last row.

Work a further 6(8:10:12) rows.

Shape top

Bind off 3 sts at beg of next 18(20:20:22) rows. *14(12:16:14) sts.*

Bind off.

NECKBAND

Join right shoulder seam.

With right side facing, size 6 (4mm) needles, pick up and k16(16:18:18) sts down left front neck to holder, then k across 34(36:38:40) sts on center front holder, pick up and k16(16:18:18) sts up right front neck to shoulder seam, k across 48(50:52:54) sts on back neck holder. *114(118:126:130) sts.*

Row 1 P2, [k2, p2] to end.

Row 2 K2, [p2, k2] to end.

Rep the last 2 rows 3 times more and row 1 again.

Bind off in rib.

FINISHING

Join left shoulder and neckband seam.

Join side seams from top of garter-st border and sleeve seams to colored threads.

Set in sleeves.

finnian

These "his and hers" vests are both knitted in Rowan
Baby Alpaca DK yarn (in two different shades of "natural
fleece-look" gray). *Baby Alpaca* makes for a warm but light
top, ideal for wearing over a shirt or blouse. The vests are
worked in seed stitch with an interesting fisherman's cable
design worked over 26 rows. The cable stitch is made up
of two basic 4-stitch cables side by side that cross over on
every 23rd pattern row. This gives the effect of the cable
changing from narrow to wide and back again.

man's vest

MEASUREMENTS

S	M	L	
To fit chest			
36–38	40–42	44–46	in
92–97	102–107	112–117	cm
Actual measurements			
Chest			
43¼	47¼	52	in
110	120	132	cm
Length to top of shoulder			
25¼	26	26¾	in
64	66	68	cm

YARN

11(12:13) x 1¾oz/109yd balls of Rowan *Baby Alpaca DK* Lincoln 209

NEEDLES

Pair each of size 3 (3.25mm) and size 6 (4mm) knitting needles
Cable needle

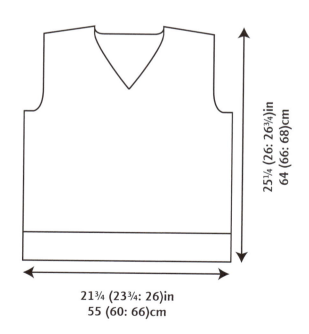

21¾ (23¾: 26)in
55 (60: 66)cm

25¼ (26: 26¾)in
64 (66: 68)cm

GAUGE

22 sts and 30 rows to 4in/10cm square over St st using size 6 (4mm) needles *or size to obtain correct gauge.*

ABBREVIATIONS

C4F—cable 4 front, slip next 2 sts on a cable needle and leave at front of work, k2, then k2 from cable needle.
C4B—cable 4 back, slip next 2 sts on a cable needle and leave at back of work, k2, then k2 from cable needle.
C8F—cable 8 front, slip next 4 sts on a cable needle and leave at front of work, k4, then k4 from cable needle.
Cr5R—cross 5 right, slip next st on a cable needle and leave at back of work, k4, then p1 from cable needle.
Cr5L—cross 5 left, slip next 4 sts on a cable needle and leave at front of work, p1, then k4 from cable needle.
S2kp—slip next 2 sts as if to k them tog, k1, then pass the 2 slipped sts over.
See also page 133.

Cable panel (worked over 14 sts)
Row 1 P2, [k4, p2] twice.
Row 2 K2, [p4, k2] twice.
Row 3 P2, C4F, p2, C4B, p2.
Row 4 As row 2.
Row 5 P2, [k4, p2] twice.
Row 6 K2, [p4, k2] twice.
Rows 7 to 18 Rep rows 1 to 6 twice more.
Row 19 P2, Cr5L, Cr5R, p2.
Row 20 K3, p8, k3.
Row 21 P3, C8F, p3.
Row 22 K3, p8, k3.
Row 23 P2, Cr5R, Cr5L, p2.
Row 24 K3, p8, k3.
These 24 rows form the cable panel and are repeated.

BACK

Using size 3 (3.25mm) needles, cast on 123(135:147) sts.

Row 1 K1, [p1, k1] to end.

Row 2 P1, [k1, p1] to end.

Rep the last 2 rows 11 times more and row 1 again.

Inc row Rib 28(31:34), * M1, [rib 1, M1] 5 times, rib 16(18:20); rep from * twice more, M1, [rib 1, M1] 5 times, rib 27(30:33). *147(159:171) sts.*

Change to size 6 (4mm) needles.

Row 1 P0(1:0), [k1, p1] 13(14:16) times, * work across row 1 of cable panel, [p1, k1] 6(7:8) times, p1; rep from * twice more, work across row 1 of cable panel, [p1, k1] 13(14:16) times, p0(1:0).

Row 2 P0(1:0), [k1, p1] 13(14:16) times, * work across row 2 of cable panel, [p1, k1] 6(7:8) times, p1; rep from * twice more, work across row 2 of cable panel, [p1, k1] 13(14:16) times, p0(1:0).

These 2 rows set the position for cable panels and form the seed st.

Cont to work in patt until back measures 16¼(16½:17) in/41(42:43)cm from cast-on edge, ending with a wrong side row.

Shape armholes

Bind off 11(12:13) sts at beg of next 2 rows. *125(135:145) sts.*

Next row Work 2 tog, patt to last 2 sts, work 2 tog.

Next row Patt to end.

Rep the last 2 rows 8(10:12) more. *107(113:119) sts **.*

Work even until back measures 24½(25¼:26) in/62(64:66)cm from cast-on edge, ending with a wrong side row.

Shape shoulders and back neck

Bind off 8(9:10) sts at beg of next 2 rows. *91(95:99) sts.*

Next row Bind off 8(9:10) sts, patt until there are 19 sts on the needle, turn and work on these sts for first side of neck.

Next row Bind off 3 sts, patt to end.

Next row Bind off 7 sts, patt to end.

Next row Bind off 3 sts, patt to end.

Bind off rem 6 sts.

With right side facing, return to rem sts, rejoin yarn, bind off center 37(39:41) sts, patt to end.

Next row Bind off 8(9:10) sts patt to end.

Next row Bind off 3 sts, patt to end.

Next row Bind off 7 sts, patt to end.

Next row Bind off 3 sts, patt to end.

Bind off rem 6 sts.

FRONT

Work as given for Back to **. *107(113:119) sts.*

Shape front neck

Next row Patt 53(56:59) turn and work on these sts for first side of neck shaping.

Next row Patt to end.

Next row Patt to last 2 sts, work 2 tog.

Rep the last 2 rows until 29(31:33) sts rem.

Work even until front measures the same as Back to shoulder, ending at armhole edge.

Shape shoulder

Bind off 8(9:10) sts at beg of next and foll right side row.

Work 1 row.

Next row Bind off 7 sts, patt to end.

Work 1 row.

Bind off rem 6 sts.

With right side facing, return to rem sts, slip center st on a holder, rejoin yarn to rem sts, patt to end.

Next row Patt to end.

Next row Work 2 tog, patt to end.

Rep the last 2 rows until 29(31:33) sts rem.

Work even until front measures the same as Back to shoulder, ending at armhole edge.

Shape shoulder

Bind off 8(9:10) sts at beg of next and foll wrong side row.

Work 1 row.

Next row Bind off 7 sts, patt to end.

Work 1 row.

Bind off rem 6 sts.

NECKBAND

Join right shoulder seam.

With right side facing, using size 3 (3.25mm) needles pick up and k56(58:60) sts down left side of front neck, k1 from center front holder, pick up and k56(58:60) sts up right side of front neck, 45(47:49) sts from around back neck. *158(164:170) sts.*

Row 1 [K1, p1] to end.
Row 2 Rib 55(57:59), s2kp, rib to end.
Row 3 [K1, p1] to end.
Row 4 Rib 54(56:58), s2kp, rib to end.
Row 5 [K1, p1] to end.
Row 6 Rib 53(55:57), s2kp, rib to end.
Row 7 [K1, p1] to end.
Row 8 Rib 52(54:56), s2kp, rib to end.
Row 9 [K1, p1] to end.
Bind off in rib, dec on this row as before.

ARMBANDS

Join left shoulder and neckband seam.
With right side facing, using size 3 (3.25mm) needles pick up and k136(142:148) sts evenly round armhole edge.
Rib row [K1, p1] to end.
Work a further 8 rows.
Bind off in rib.

FINISHING

Join side and armband seams.

woman's vest

MEASUREMENTS

	S	M	L	
To fit bust				
	32–34	36–38	40–42	in
	82–87	92–97	102–107	cm
Actual measurements				
Bust				
	35	39½	43½	in
	89	100	110	cm
Length to top of shoulder				
	20	20¾	21½	in
	51	53	55	cm

YARN

8(9:10) x 1¾oz/109yd balls of Rowan *Baby Alpaca DK* Southdown 208

NEEDLES

Pair each of size 3 (3.25mm) and size 6 (4mm) knitting needles
Cable needle

GAUGE

22 sts and 30 rows to 4in/10cm square over St st using size 6 (4mm) needles *or size to obtain correct gauge.*

ABBREVIATIONS

C4F—cable 4 front, slip next 2 sts on a cable needle and leave at front of work, k2, then k2 from cable needle.

C4B—cable 4 back, slip next 2 sts on a cable needle and leave at back of work, k2, then k2 from cable needle.

C8F—cable 8 front, slip next 4 sts on a cable needle and leave at front of work, k4, then k4 from cable needle.

Cr5R—cross 5 right, slip next st on a cable needle and leave at back of work, k4, then p1 from cable needle.

Cr5L—cross 5 left, slip next 4 sts on a cable needle and leave at front of work, p1, then k4 from cable needle.

See also page 133.

Cable panel (worked over 14 sts)
Row 1 P2, [k4, p2] twice.
Row 2 K2, [p4, k2] twice.
Row 3 P2, C4F, p2, C4B, p2.
Row 4 As row 2.
Row 5 P2, [k4, p2] twice.
Row 6 K2, [p4, k2] twice.
Rows 7 to 18 Rep rows 1 to 6 twice more.
Row 19 P2, Cr5L, Cr5R, p2.
Row 20 K3, p8, k3.
Row 21 P3, C8F, p3.
Row 22 K3, p8, k3.
Row 23 P2, Cr5R, Cr5L, p2.
Row 24 K3, p8, k3.
These 24 rows form the cable panel and are repeated.

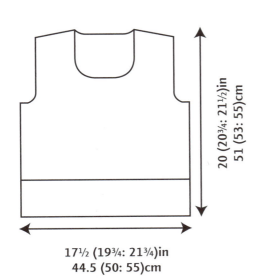

20 (20¾: 21½)in
51 (53: 55)cm

17½ (19¾: 21¾)in
44.5 (50: 55)cm

BACK

Using size 3 (3.25mm) needles, cast on
99(111:123) sts.

Row 1 K1, [p1, k1] to end.

Row 2 P1, [k1, p1] to end.

Rep the last 2 rows 14 times more and row 1 again.

Inc row Rib 22(25:28), * M1, [rib 1, M1] 5 times, rib
12(14:16); rep from * twice more, M1, [rib 1, M1] 5
times, rib 21(24:27). *123(135:147) sts.*

Change to size 6 (4mm) needles.

Row 1 P0(1:0), [k1, p1] 10(11:13) times, * work across
row 1 of cable panel, [p1, k1] 4(5:6) times, p1; rep
from * twice more, work across row 1 of cable panel,
[p1, k1] 10(11:13) times, p0(1:0).

Row 2 P0(1:0), [k1, p1] 10(11:13) times, * work across
row 2 of cable panel, [p1, k1] 4(5:6) times, p1; rep
from * twice more, work across row 2 of cable panel,
[p1, k1] 10(11:13) times, p0(1:0).

These 2 rows set the position for cable panels and
form the seed st.

Cont to work in patt until back measures 12¼(12½:13)
in/31(32:33)cm from cast-on edge, ending with a
wrong side row.

Shape armholes

Bind off 9(10:11) sts at beg of next 2 rows.
105(115:125) sts.

Next row Work 2 tog, patt to last 2 sts, work 2 tog.

Next row Patt to end.

Rep the last 2 rows 6(8:10) more. *91(97:103) sts **.*
Work even until back measures 19¼(20:20¾)in/
49(51:53)cm from cast-on edge, ending with a wrong
side row.

Shape shoulders and back neck

Bind off 6(7:8) sts at beg of next 2 rows. *79(83:87) sts.*

Next row Bind off 6(7:8) sts, patt until there are 18 sts
on the needle, turn and work on these sts for first side
of neck.

Next row Bind off 3 sts, patt to end.

Next row Bind off 6 sts, patt to end.

Next row Bind off 3 sts, patt to end.

Bind off rem 6 sts.

With right side facing, return to rem sts, rejoin yarn,
bind off center 31(33:35) sts, patt to end.

Next row Bind off 6(7:8) sts patt to end.

Next row Bind off 3 sts, patt to end.

Next row Bind off 6 sts, patt to end.

Next row Bind off 3 sts, patt to end.

Bind off rem 6 sts.

FRONT

Work as given for Back to **.

Shape front neck

Next row Patt 35(37:39) turn and work on these sts
for first side of neck shaping.

Next row Patt to end.

Next row Patt to last 2 sts, work 2 tog.

Rep the last 2 rows until 24(26:28) sts rem.

Work even until front measures the same as Back to
shoulder, ending at armhole edge.

Shape shoulder

Bind off 6(7:8) sts at beg of next and foll right side row.

Work 1 row.

Next row Bind off 6 sts, patt to end.

Work 1 row.

Bind off rem 6 sts.

With right side facing, return to rem sts, slip center
21(23:25) sts on a holder, rejoin yarn, patt to end.

Next row Patt to end.

Next row Work 2 tog, patt to end.

Rep the last 2 rows until 24(26:28) sts rem.

Work even until front measures the same as back to
shoulder, ending at armhole edge.

Shape shoulder

Bind off 6(7:8) sts at beg of next and foll wrong side
row.

Work 1 row.

Next row Bind off 6 sts, patt to end.

Work 1 row.

Bind off rem 6 sts.

NECKBAND

Join right shoulder seam.

With right side facing, using size 3 (3.25mm) needles
pick up and k40 sts down left side of front neck,

k21(23:25) sts from center front holder, pick up and k40 sts up right side of front neck, 35(37:39) sts from around back neck. *136(140:144) sts.*
Rib row [K1, p1] to end.
Work a further 5 rows.
Bind off in rib.

ARMBANDS

Join left shoulder and neckband seam.
With right side facing, using size 3 (3.25mm) needles pick up and k122(128:134) sts evenly round armhole edge.
Rib row [K1, p1] to end.
Work a further 5 rows.
Bind off in rib.

FINISHING

Join side and armband seams.

hamish

This snug pull-on hat is knitted in Rowan *British Sheep Breeds DK*, which gives crisp definition to the textured medallion seed-stitch cable pattern while being cozy and warm to wear. The medallion cable pattern is worked over a 24-row pattern repeat, separated by bands of stockinette stitch. Extra care and attention is needed in shaping the crown and in order to give a neat finish. The hat has a neat short and elastic k1, p1 ribbed brim.

FINISHED SIZE

To fit an average size head.

YARN

2 x 1¾oz/131yd balls of Rowan *British Sheep Breeds DK* Mid Brown Bluefaced Leicester 782

NEEDLES

Pair each of size 3 (3.25mm) and size 6 (4mm) knitting needles
Cable needle

GAUGE

22 sts and 30 rows to 4in/10cm square over St st using size 6 (4mm) needles *or size to obtain correct gauge*.

32 sts and 30 rows to 4in/10cm square over cable patt using size 6 (4mm) needles *or size to obtain correct gauge*.

ABBREVIATIONS

C8R—cross 8 right slip next 4 sts on a cable needle and leave at back of work, [k1, p1] twice, then k4 from cable needle.

C8L—cross 8 left slip next 4 sts on a cable needle and leave at front of work, k4, then [k1, p1] twice from cable needle. See also page 133.

BEANIE

Using size 3 (3.25mm) needles, cast on 172 sts.
Rib row 1 [K1, p1] to end.
Rep this row for 1½in/4cm.
Change to size 6 (4mm) needles.
Cont in patt.
Row 1 (rs) * P3, C8R, C8L, p3, k3; rep from * to last 22 sts, p3, C8R, C8L, p3.
Row 2 * K3, [p1, k1] twice, p9, k1, p1, k4, p3; rep from * to last 22 sts, k3, [p1, k1] twice, p9, k1, p1, k4.
Row 3 * P3, [k1, p1] twice, k9, p1, k1, p4, k3; rep from * to last 22 sts, p3, [k1, p1] twice, k9, p1, k1, p4.
Row 4 * K3, [p1, k1] twice, p9, k1, p1, k4, p3; rep from * to last 22 sts, k3, [p1, k1] twice, p9, k1, p1, k4.

Rows 5 to 10 Rep rows 3 and 4 three times.
Row 11 * P3, C8L, C8R, p3, k3; rep from * to last 22 sts, p3, C8L, C8R, p3.
Row 12 * K3, p4, [p1, k1] 4 times, p4, k3, p3; rep from * to last 22 sts, k3, p4, [p1, k1] 4 times, p4, k3.
Row 13 * P3, k4, [k1, p1] 4 times, k4, p3, k3; rep from * to last 22 sts, p3, k4, [k1, p1] 4 times, k4, p3,
Row 14 * K3, p4, [p1, k1] 4 times, p4, k3, p3; rep from * to last 22 sts, k3, p4, [p1, k1] 4 times, p4, k3.
Rows 15 to 24 Rep rows 13 and 14 five times more. These 24 rows form the patt.
Work a further 24 rows, ending with row 24.
Row 1 dec (rs) * P3, slip next 4 sts on a cable needle and leave at back of work, [k1, p1] twice, then [k2tog] twice from cable needle, slip next 4 sts on a cable needle and leave at front of work, [k2tog] twice, then [k1, p1] twice from cable needle, p3, k3; rep from * to last 22 sts, p3, slip next 4 sts on a cable needle and leave at back of work, [k1, p1] twice then [k2tog] twice from cable needle, slip next 4 sts on a cable needle and leave at front of work, [k2tog] twice, then [k1, p1] twice from cable needle, p3. *144 sts.*
Row 2 * K3, [p1, k1] twice, p5, k1, p1, k4, p3; rep from * to last 18 sts, k3, [p1, k1] twice, p5, k1, p1, k4.
Row 3 * P1, p2tog, [k1, p1] twice, [k2tog] twice, [k1, p1] twice, p1, p2tog, k3; rep from * to last 18 sts, p1, p2tog, [k1, p1] twice, [k2tog] twice, [k1, p1] twice, p2tog, p1. *116 sts.*
Row 4 * K2, [p1, k1] twice, p3, k1, p1, k3, p3; rep from * to last 14 sts, k2, [p1, k1] twice, p3, k1, p1, k3.
Row 5 * P2tog, [k1, p1] twice, k2tog, [k1, p1] twice, p2tog, k1, k2tog; rep from * to last 14 sts, p2tog, [k1, p1] twice, k2tog, [k1, p1] twice, p2tog. *89 sts.*
Row 6 * K1, [p1, k1] twice, p2tog, k1, p1, k2tog, p2tog; rep from * to last 11 sts, k1, [p1, k1] twice, p2tog, k1, p1, k2tog. *69 sts.*
Row 7 K1, [p1, k1] to end.
Row 8 K3tog, [p3tog, k3tog] 11 times.
Break off yarn, thread through rem sts, and fasten off.

FINISHING

Join seam.

inisheer

Another "his and hers" set, this time knitted in Rowan *Lima* with a great traditional nautical cable rope Aran design on the front and back panel of the sweaters, set into seed stitch. The big interlacing knot cable forms the central panel, with smaller cables to each side. A twisted cable forms the finish for the collar, cuffs, and welt.

man's sweater

MEASUREMENTS

	S	M	L	
To fit chest				
	38–42	44–48	50–54	in
	97–107	112–122	127–137	cm
Actual measurements				
Chest				
	48	54½	60½	in
	122	138	154	cm
Length to top of shoulder				
	26¾	27½	28¼	in
	68	70	72	cm
Sleeve length				
	20½in/52cm			

YARN

21(23:25) x 1¾oz/109yd balls of Rowan *Lima*
Patagonia 878

NEEDLES

Pair each of size 7 (4.5mm) and size 9 (5.5mm)
knitting needles
Cable needle

GAUGE

20 sts and 26 rows to 4in/10cm square over St st
using size 9 (5.5mm) needles *or size to obtain correct
gauge*.
20 sts and 32 rows to 4in/10cm square over seed st
using size 9 (5.5mm) needles *or size to obtain correct
gauge*.
Center panel measures 7½in/19cm wide.

ABBREVIATIONS

C4B—cable 4 back, slip next 2 sts on a cable needle
and leave at back of work, k2, then k2 from cable
needle.
C6F—cable 6 front, slip next 3 sts on a cable needle
and leave at front of work, k3, then k3 from cable
needle.

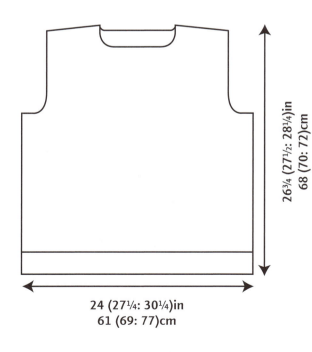

24 (27¼: 30¼)in
61 (69: 77)cm

26¾ (27½: 28¼)in
68 (70: 72)cm

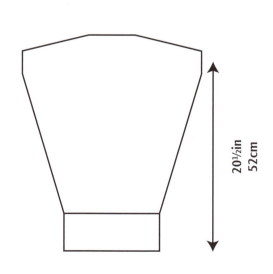

20½in
52cm

C6B—cable 6 back, slip next 3 sts on a cable needle and leave at back of work, k3, then k3 from cable needle.

C12F—cable 12 front, slip next 6 sts on a cable needle and leave at front of work, k6, then k6 from cable needle.

C12B—cable 12 back, slip next 6 sts on a cable needle and leave at back of work, k6, then k6 from cable needle.

Cr8R—cross 8 right, slip next 2 sts on a cable needle and leave at back of work, k6, then p2 from cable needle.

Cr8L—cross 8 left, slip next 6 sts on a cable needle and leave at front of work, p2, then k6 from cable needle.

See also page 133.

Cable panel A (worked over 13 sts)
Row 1 P2, k9, p2.
Row 2 K2, p9, k2.
Row 3 P2, C6B, k3, p2.
Row 4 As row 2.
Row 5 P2, k9, p2.
Row 6 K2, p9, k2.
Row 7 P2, k3, C6F, p2.
Row 8 K2, p9, k2.
These 8 rows form the cable panel and are repeated.

Cable panel B (worked over 36 sts)
Row 1 K6, p6, k12, p6, k6.
Row 2 P6, k6, p12, k6, p6.
Row 3 K6, p6, C12B, p6, k6.
Row 4 As row 2.
Row 5 K6, p4, Cr8R, Cr8L, p4, k6.
Row 6 P6, [k4, p6] 3 times.
Row 7 K6, p2, Cr8R, p4, Cr8L, p2, k6.
Row 8 P6, k2, p6, k8, p6, k2, p6.
Row 9 K6, Cr8R, p8, Cr8L, k6.
Row 10 P12, k12, p12.
Row 11 C12B, p12, C12F.
Row 12 P12, k12, p12.
Row 13 K12, p12, k12.

Rows 14 to 16 Rep rows 12 and 13 once and row 12 again.
Rows 17 and 18 As rows 11 and 12.
Row 19 K6, Cr8L, p8, Cr8R, k6.
Row 20 As row 8.
Row 21 K6, p2, Cr8L, p4, Cr8R, p2, k6.
Row 22 As row 6.
Row 23 K6, p4, Cr8L, Cr8R, p4, k6.
Row 24 As row 4.
Row 25 K6, p6, C12B, p6, k6.
Row 26 As row 2.
Row 27 As row 1.
Row 28 As row 2.
These 28 rows form the cable panel and are repeated.

BACK
Using size 7 (4.5mm) needles, cast on 182(206:230) sts.
Row 1 P2, [k4, p2] to end.
Row 2 K2, [p4, k2] to end.
Row 3 P2, [C4B, p2] to end.
Row 4 As row 2.
Rows 5 to 14 Rep rows 1 to 4 twice more and rows 1 and 2 again.
Row 15 P2, * slip next 2 sts on a cable needle and leave at back of work, [k next st tog with first st on cable needle] twice, p2; rep from * to end. *122(138:154) sts.*
Row 16 K2, [p2, k2] to end.
Change to size 9 (5.5mm) needles.
Seed st row 1 [K1, p1] to end.
Seed st row 2 [P1, k1] to end.
These 2 rows form the seed st.
Cont in seed st until back measures 17¼(17¾:18)in/ 44(45:46)cm from cast-on edge, ending with a wrong side row.
Shape armholes
Bind off 6(8:10) sts at beg of next 2 rows. *110(122:134) sts.*
Next row Work 2tog, patt to last 2 sts, work 2tog.
Next row Patt to end.
Rep the last 2 rows 6(8:10) more. *96(104:112) sts.*

Work even until back measures 26¼(27¼:28)in/ 67(69:71)cm from cast-on edge, ending with a wrong side row.

Shape shoulders and back neck

Bind off 7(8:9) sts at beg of next 2 rows. *82(88:94) sts.*

Next row Bind off 7(8:9) sts, patt until there are 18(19:20) sts on the needle, turn and work on these sts for first side of neck.

Next row Bind off 2 sts, patt to end.

Next row Bind off 7(8:9) sts, patt to end.

Next row Bind off 2 sts, patt to end.

Bind off rem 7 sts.

With right side facing, return to rem sts rejoin yarn, bind off center 32(34:36) sts, patt to end.

Next row Bind off 7(8:9) sts patt to end.

Next row Bind off 2 sts, patt to end.

Next row Bind off 7(8:9) sts, patt to end.

Next row Bind off 2 sts, patt to end.

Bind off rem 7 sts.

FRONT

Using size 7 (4.5mm) needles, cast on 182(206:230) sts.

Row 1 P2, [k4, p2] to end.

Row 2 K2, [p4, k2] to end.

Row 3 P2, [C4B, p2] to end.

Row 4 As row 2.

Rows 5 to 14 Rep rows 1 to 4 twice more and rows 1 and 2 again.

Row 15 * P2, slip next 2 sts on a cable needle and leave at back of work, [k next st tog with first st on cable needle] twice; rep from * 9(11:13) times more, patt 62 sts, **, slip next 2 sts on a cable needle and leave at back of work, [k next st tog with first st on cable needle] twice p2; rep from ** 9(11:13) times more. *142(158:174) sts.*

Row 16 K2, [p2, k2], 10(12:14) times, patt 58, [k2, p2] 10(12:14) times, k2.

Change to size 9 (5.5mm) needles.

Row 1 [K1, p1] 20(24:28) times, work across row 1 of Panel A, Panel B and Panel A, [k1, p1] 20(24:28) times.

Row 2 [P1, k1] 20(24:28) times, work across row 2 of Panel A, Panel B and Panel A, [p1, k1] 20(24:28) times. These 2 rows form the seed st and set the positions for the cable panels.

Cont in patt until front measures 17¼(17¾:18)in/ 44(45:46)cm from cast on edge, ending with a wrong side row.

Shape armholes

Bind off 6(8:10) sts at beg of next 2 rows. *130(142:154) sts.*

Next row Work 2tog, patt to last 2 sts, work 2tog.

Next row Patt to end.

Rep the last 2 rows 6(8:10) more. *116(124:132) sts.* Work even until front measures 24¼(24¾:25¼)in/ 62(63:64)cm from cast-on edge, ending with a wrong side row.

Shape front neck

Next row Patt 37(41:45), turn and work on these sts for first side of neck shaping.

Next row Bind off 3(4:5), patt to end.

Next row Patt to end.

Next row Bind off 2 sts, patt to end.

Rep the last 2 rows once more.

Next row Patt to last 2 sts, work 2 tog. *30(33:36) sts.*

Next row Patt to end.

Next row Patt to last 2 sts, work 2 tog. *28(31:34) sts.* Work even until front measures the same as back to shoulder, ending at armhole edge.

Shape shoulder

Bind off 7(8:9) sts at beg of next and 2 foll right side rows.

Work 1 row.

Bind off rem 7 sts.

With right side facing, return to rem sts, rejoin yarn, slip center 42 sts on a holder, patt to end.

Next row Patt to end.

Next row Bind off 3(4:5), patt to end.

Next row Patt to end.

Next row Bind off 2 sts, patt to end.

Rep the last 2 rows once more.

Next row Patt to last 2 sts, work 2 tog.

Next row Patt to end.

Next row Patt to last 2 sts, work 2 tog. *28(31:34) sts.*

Work even until front measures the same as back to shoulder, ending at armhole edge.

Shape shoulder

Bind off 7(8:9) sts at beg of next and 2 foll wrong side rows.

Work 1 row.

Bind off rem 7 sts.

SLEEVES

Using size 7 (4.5mm) needles, cast on 74(80:86) sts.

Row 1 P2, [k4, p2] to end.

Row 2 K2, [p4, k2] to end.

Row 3 P2, [C4B, p2] to end.

Row 4 As row 2.

Rows 5 to 18 Rep rows 1 to 4 three times more and rows 1 and 2 again.

Row 19 P2, * slip next 2 sts on a cable needle and leave at back of work, [k next st tog with first st on cable needle] twice, p2; rep from * to end. *50(54:58) sts.*

Row 20 K2, [p2, k2] to end.

Change to size 9 (5.5mm) needles.

Seed st row 1 [K1, p1] to end.

Seed st row 2 [P1, k1] to end.

These 2 rows form the seed st.

Inc row Inc in first st, patt to end.

Work 2 rows.

Rep the last 3 rows 42 times more and the inc row again. *94(98:102) sts.*

Cont even until sleeve measures 20½in/52cm, from cast-on edge, ending with a wrong side row.

Place markers at each end of last row.

Work a further 8(10:12) rows.

Shape top

Bind off 3 sts at beg of next 24 rows. *22(26:30) sts.*

Bind off.

NECKBAND

Join right shoulder seam.

With right side facing, size 9 (5.5mm) needles, pick up and k21(26:31) sts down left front neck to holder, then patt across 42 sts on center front holder, pick up and k20(25:30) sts up right front neck to shoulder seam, 46(51:56) sts around back neck. *129(144:159) sts.*

Row 1 (ws) [K2, p3] 13(15:17) times, k1, patt 42, k1, [p3, k2] 4(5:6) times.

Row 2 P2, [k1, M1, k2, p2] 4(5:6) times, k4, [p2, k4] 6 times, [p2, k1, M1, k2] 13(15:17) times, p2. *146(164:182) sts.*

Row 3 K2, [p4, k2] to end.

Row 4 P2, [C4B, p2] to end.

Row 5 K2, [p4, k2] to end.

Row 6 P2, [k4, p4] to end.

Row 7 K2, [p4, k2] to end.

Rows 8 to 15 Rep rows 4 to 7 twice more.

Change to size 7 (4.5mm) needles.

Rows 16 to 23 Rep rows 4 to 7 twice more.

Row 24 P2, * slip next 2 sts on a cable needle and leave at back of work, [k next st tog with first st on cable needle] twice, p2; rep from * to end. *98(110:122) sts.*

Bind off in rib.

FINISHING

Join left shoulder and neckband. Join side and sleeve seams. Set in sleeves.

woman's sweater

MEASUREMENTS

	XS	S	M	L	XL	
To fit bust						
	32–34	34–36	36–38	38–40	40–42	in
	82–87	87–92	92–97	97–102	102–107	cm
Actual measurements						
Bust						
	38½	41¾	44¾	48	51¼	in
	98	106	114	122	130	cm
Length to top of shoulder						
	20	20½	20¾	21¼	21¾	in
	51	52	53	54	55	cm
Sleeve length						
17¾in/45cm						

YARN

13(14:15:16:17) x 1¾oz/109yd balls of Rowan *Lima* Andes 880

NEEDLES

Pair each of size 7 (4.5mm) and size 9 (5.5mm) knitting needles
Cable needle

GAUGE

20 sts and 26 rows to 4in/10cm square over St st using size 9 (5.5mm) needles *or size to obtain correct gauge.*

20 sts and 32 rows to 4in/10cm square over seed st using size 9 (5.5mm) needles *or size to obtain correct gauge.*

Center panel measures 7½in/19cm wide.

ABBREVIATIONS

C4B—cable 4 back, slip next 2 sts on a cable needle and leave at back of work, k2, then k2 from cable needle.

C6F—cable 6 front, slip next 3 sts on a cable needle and leave at front of work, k3, then k3 from cable needle.

C6B—cable 6 back, slip next 3 sts on a cable needle and leave at back of work, k3, then k3 from cable needle.

C12F—cable 12 front, slip next 6 sts on a cable needle and leave at front of work, k6, then k6 from cable needle.

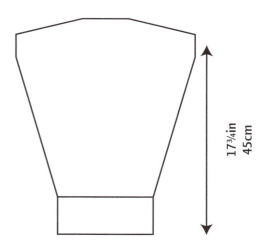

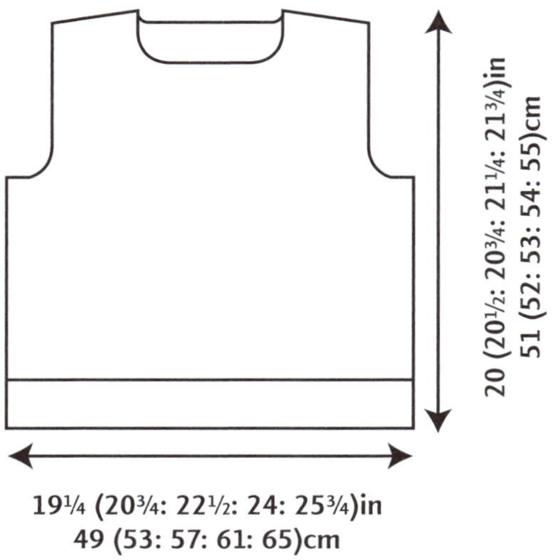

20 (20½: 20¾: 21¼: 21¾)in
51 (52: 53: 54: 55)cm

19¼ (20¾: 22½: 24: 25¾)in
49 (53: 57: 61: 65)cm

17¾in
45cm

C12B — cable 12 back, slip next 6 sts on a cable needle and leave at back of work, k6, then k6 from cable needle.

Cr8R — cross 8 right, slip next 2 sts on a cable needle and leave at back of work, k6, then p2 from cable needle.

Cr8L — cross 8 left, slip next 6 sts on a cable needle and leave at front of work, p2, then k6 from cable needle.

See also page 133.

Cable panel A (worked over 13 sts)
Row 1 P2, k9, p2.
Row 2 K2, p9, k2.
Row 3 P2, C6B, k3, p2.
Row 4 As row 2.
Row 5 P2, k9, p2.
Row 6 K2, p9, k2.
Row 7 P2, k3, C6F, p2.
Row 8 K2, p9, k2.
These 8 rows form cable panel A and are repeated.

Cable panel B (worked over 36 sts)
Row 1 K6, p6, k12, p6, k6.
Row 2 P6, k6, p12, k6, p6.
Row 3 K6, p6, C12B, p6, k6.
Row 4 As row 2.
Row 5 K6, p4, Cr8R, Cr8L, p4, k6.
Row 6 P6, [k4, p6] 3 times.
Row 7 K6, p2, Cr8R, p4, Cr8L, p2, k6.
Row 8 P6, k2, p6, k8, p6, k2, p6.
Row 9 K6, Cr8R, p8, Cr8L, k6.
Row 10 P12, k12, p12.
Row 11 C12B, p12, C12F.
Row 12 P12, k12, p12.
Row 13 K12, p12, k12.
Rows 14 to 16 Rep rows 12 and 13 once and row 12 again.
Rows 17 and 18 As rows 11 and 12.
Row 19 K6, Cr8L, p8, Cr8R, k6.
Row 20 As row 8.
Row 21 K6, p2, Cr8L, p4, Cr8R, p2, k6.

Row 22 As row 6.
Row 23 K6, p4, Cr8L, Cr8R, p4, k6.
Row 24 As row 4.
Row 25 K6, p6, C12B, p6, k6.
Row 26 As row 2.
Row 27 As row 1.
Row 28 As row 2.
These 28 rows form cable panel B and are repeated.

BACK
Using size 7 (4.5mm) needles, cast on 146(158:170:182:194) sts.
Row 1 P2, [k4, p2] to end.
Row 2 K2, [p4, k2] to end.
Row 3 P2, [C4B, p2] to end.
Row 4 As row 2.
Rows 5 to 18 Rep rows 1 to 4 three times more and rows 1 and 2 again.
Row 19 P2, * slip next 2 sts on a cable needle and leave at back of work, [k next st tog with first st on cable needle] twice, p2; rep from * to end. *98(106:114:122:130) sts.*
Row 20 K2, [p2, k2] to end.
Change to size 9 (5.5mm) needles.
Seed st row 1 [K1, p1] to end.
Seed st row 2 [P1, k1] to end.
These 2 rows form the seed st.
Cont in seed st until back measures 12¼(12½:12½:13: 13)in/31(32:32:33:33)cm from cast-on edge, ending with a wrong side row.
Shape armholes
Bind off 5(6:6:7:7) sts at beg of next 2 rows. *88(94:102:108:116) sts.*
Next row Work 2tog, patt to last 2 sts, work 2tog.
Next row Patt to end.
Rep the last 2 rows 4(4:5:5:6) times more. *78(84:90:96:102) sts.*
Work even until back measures 19¾(20:20½:20¾: 21¼)in/50(51:52:53:54)cm from cast-on edge, ending with a wrong side row.
Shape shoulders and back neck
Bind off 5 sts at beg of next 2 rows.

68(74:80:86:92) sts.
Next row Bind off 5 sts, patt until there are
16(18:20:22:24) sts on the needle, turn and work on
these sts for first side of neck.
Next row Bind off 2 sts, patt to end.
Next row Bind off 6(7:8:9:10) sts, patt to end.
Next row Bind off 2 sts, patt to end.
Bind off rem 6(7:8:9:10) sts.
With right side facing, return to rem sts rejoin yarn,
bind off center 26(28:30:32:34) sts, patt to end.
Next row Bind off 5 sts patt to end.
Next row Bind off 2 sts, patt to end.
Next row Bind off 6(7:8:9:10) sts, patt to end.
Next row Bind off 2 sts, patt to end.
Bind off rem 6(7:8:9:10) sts.

FRONT

Using size 7 (4.5mm) needles, cast on
146(158:170:182:194) sts.
Row 1 P2, [k4, p2] to end.
Row 2 K2, [p4, k2] to end.
Row 3 P2, [C4B, p2] to end.
Row 4 As row 2.
Rows 5 to 18 Rep rows 1 to 4 three times more and
rows 1 and 2 again.
Row 19 * P2, slip next 2 sts on a cable needle and
leave at back of work, [k next st tog with first st on
cable needle] twice; rep from * 6(7:8:9:10) times
more, patt 62 sts, **, slip next 2 sts on a cable needle
and leave at back of work, [k next st tog with first st on
cable needle] twice p2; rep from ** 6(7:8:9:10) times
more. 118(126:134:142:150) sts.
Row 20 K2, [p2, k2] 7(8:9:10:11) times, patt 58, [k2,
p2] 7(8:9:10:11) times, k2.
Change to size 9 (5.5mm) needles.
Row 1 [K1, p1] 14(16:18:20:22) times, work across
row 1 of Panel A, Panel B, and Panel A, [k1, p1]
14(16:18:20:22) times.
Row 2 [P1, k1] 14(16:18:20:22) times, work across
row 2 of Panel A, Panel B, and Panel A, [p1, k1]
14(16:18:20:22) times.
These 2 rows form the seed st and set the positions for

the cable panels.
Cont in patt until front measures 12¼(12½:12½:13:13)
in/31(32:32:33:33)cm from cast-on edge, ending with
a wrong side row.
Shape armholes
Bind off 5(6:6:7:7) sts at beg of next 2 rows.
108(114:122:128:136) sts.
Next row Work 2tog, patt to last 2 sts, work 2tog.
Next row Patt to end.
Rep the last 2 rows 4(4:5:5:6) times more.
98(104:110:116:122) sts.
Work even until front measures 17¾(18:18½:18¾:
19¼)in45(46:47:48:49)cm from cast-on edge, ending
with a wrong side row.
Shape front neck
Next row Patt 28(31:34:37:40), turn and work on
these sts for first side of neck shaping.
Next row Bind off 2(3:4:5:6), patt to end.
Next row Patt to end.
Next row Work 2tog, patt to end.
Next row Patt to end.
Rep the last 2 rows 3 times more. 22(24:26:28:30) sts.
Work even until front measures the same as back to
shoulder, ending at armhole edge.
Shape shoulder
Bind off 5 sts at beg of next and foll right side row.
Work 1 row.
Next row Bind off 6(7:8:9:10) sts, patt to end.
Work 1 row.
Bind off rem 6(7:8:9:10) sts.
With right side facing, return to rem sts rejoin yarn, slip
center 42 sts on a holder, patt to end.
Next row Patt to end.
Next row Bind off 2(3:4:5:6), patt to end.
Next row Patt to end.
Next row Work 2 tog, patt to end.
Next row Patt to end.
Rep the last 2 rows 3 times more. 22(24:26:28:30) sts.
Work even until front measures the same as back to
shoulder, ending at armhole edge.
Shape shoulder
Bind off 5 sts at beg of next and foll wrong side row.

Work 1 row.
Next row Bind off 6(7:8:9:10) sts, patt to end.
Work 1 row.
Bind off rem 6(7:8:9:10) sts.

SLEEVES

Using size 7 (4.5mm) needles, cast on
62(68:68:74:74) sts.
Row 1 P2, [k4, p2] to end.
Row 2 K2, [p4, k2] to end.
Row 3 P2, [C4B, p2] to end.
Row 4 As row 2.
Rows 5 to 18 Rep rows 1 to 4 three times more and
rows 1 and 2 again.
Row 19 P2, * slip next 2 sts on a cable needle
and leave at back of work, [k next st tog with first
st on cable needle] twice, p2; rep from * to end.
42(46:46:50:50) sts.
Row 20 K2, [p2, k2] to end.
Change to size 9 (5.5mm) needles.
Seed st row 1 [K1, p1] to end.
Seed st row 2 [P1, k1] to end.
These 2 rows form the seed st.
Inc row Inc in first st, patt to end.
Work 2 rows.
Rep the last 3 rows 32 times more and the inc row
again. *76(80:80:84:84) sts.*
Cont even until sleeve measures 17¾in/45cm, from
cast-on edge, ending with a wrong side row.
Place markers at each end of last row.
Work a further 6(8:8:10:10) rows.
Shape top
Bind off 3 sts at beg of next 20 rows.
16(20:20:24:24) sts.
Bind off.

NECKBAND

Join right shoulder seam.
With right side facing, size 9 (5.5mm) needles, pick
up and k21(21:26:26:26) sts down left front neck to
holder, then patt across 42 sts on center front holder,
pick up and k20(20:25:25:25) sts up right front neck to

shoulder seam, 36(36:41:41:46) sts around back neck.
119(119:134:134:139) sts.
Row 1 (ws) [K2, p3] 11(11:13:13:14) times, k1, patt
42, k1, [p3, k2] 4(4:5:5:5) times.
Row 2 P2, [k1, M1, k2, p2] 4(4:5:5:5) times, k4, [p2,
k4] 6 times, [p2, k1, M1, k2] 11(11:13:13:14) times,
p2. *134(134:152:152:158) sts.*
Row 3 K2, [p4, k2] to end.
Row 4 P2, [C4B, p2] to end.
Row 5 K2, [p4, k2] to end.
Row 6 P2, [k4, p4] to end.
Row 7 K2, [p4, k2] to end.
Rows 8 to 15 Rep rows 4 to 7 twice more.
Change to size 7 (4.5mm) needles.
Rows 16 to 23 Rep rows 4 to 7 twice more.
Row 24 P2, * slip next 2 sts on a cable needle
and leave at back of work, [k next st tog with first
st on cable needle] twice, p2; rep from * to end.
90(90:102:102:106) sts.
Bind off in rib.

FINISHING

Join left shoulder and neckband. Join side and sleeve
seams. Set in sleeves.

iona

Knitted in Rowan *Lima*, with its high percentage of baby alpaca yarn, this soft but cozy pull-on hat is made up of beautifully textured 6-stitch plait cables with simple to work 10-stitch lace twist cables in between. A very effective "winding-wave" texture is achieved by the lace twist stitch. The hat has a deep k2, p2 rib brim, which is folded over for extra warmth.

FINISHED SIZE

To fit an average size head.

YARN

2 x 1¾oz/109yd balls of Rowan *Lima* Peru 889

NEEDLES

Pair each of size 8 (5mm) and size 9 (5.5mm) knitting needles
Cable needle

GAUGE

25 sts and 25 rows to 4in/10cm over patt using size 9 (5.5mm) needles *or size to obtain correct gauge*.

ABBREVIATIONS

C4B—cable 4 back, slip next 2 sts on a cable needle and leave at back of work, k2, then k2 from cable needle.
C4F—cable 4 front, slip next 2 sts on a cable needle and leave at front of work, k2, then k2 from cable needle.
See also page 133.

HAT

Using size 9 (5.5mm) needles, cast on 122 sts.
Row 1 (rs) P2, [k2, p2] to end.
Row 2 K2, [p2, k2] to end.
Rep the last 2 rows for 2in/5cm, ending with row 2.
Change to size 8 (5mm) needles.
Work a further 2in/5cm, ending row 2.
Change to size 9 (5.5mm) needles.
Cont in patt.
Row 1 P2, [k5, k2tog, k3, yo, p2, C4F, k2, p2] to end.
Row 2 and every foll wrong side row K2, [p6, k2, p10, k2] to end.
Row 3 P2, [k4, k2tog, k3, yo, k1, p2, k2, C4B, p2] to end.
Row 5 P2, [k3, k2tog, k3, yo, k2, p2, C4F, k2, p2] to end.
Row 7 P2, [k2, k2tog, k3, yo, k3, p2, k2, C4B, p2] to end.

Row 9 P2, [k1, k2tog, k3, yo, k4, p2, C4F, k2, p2] to end.
Row 11 P2, [k2tog, k3, yo, k5, p2, k2, C4B, p2] to end.
Row 12 As row 2.
Rows 13 to 24 As rows 1 to 12.
Row 25 P2, [yo, k3, skp, k5, p2, C4F, k2, p2] to end.
Row 26 and every foll wrong side row K2, [p6, k2, p10, k2] to end.
Row 27 P2, [k1, yo, k3, skp, k4, p2, k2, C4B, p2] to end.
Row 29 P2, [k2, yo, k3, skp, k3, p2, C4F, k2, p2] to end.
Row 31 P2, [k3, yo, k3, skp, k2, p2, k2, C4B, p2] to end.
Row 33 P2, [k4, yo, k3, skp, k1, p2, C4F, k2, p2] to end.
Row 35 P2, [k5, yo, k3, skp, p2, k2, C4B p2] to end.
Row 37 P2, [k3, skp, k5, p2, C4F, k2, p2] to end.
Row 38 K2, [p6, k2, p9, k2] to end.
Row 39 P2, [k3, skp, k4, p2, k2, C4B, p2] to end.
Row 40 K2, [p6, k2, p8, k2] to end.
Row 41 P2, [k3, skp, k3, p2, C4F, k2, p2] to end.
Row 42 K2, [p6, k2, p7, k2] to end.
Row 43 P2, [k3, skp, k2, p2, k2, C4B, p2] to end.
Row 44 K2, [p6, k2, p6, k2] to end.
Row 45 P2, * k3, skp, k1, p2, slip next 2 sts on a cable needle and leave at front of work, [sl 1 from cable needle, k next st, psso] twice, k2tog, p2; rep from * to end.
Row 46 K2, [p2tog, p1, k2tog, p2tog, tbl, p1, p2tog k2tog] to end.
Row 47 [P1, k3tog tbl, k3tog] to last 2 sts, p2tog.
Row 48 K1, [p2tog, k1] to end.
Row 49 [K2tog] to last st, p1.
Leaving a long end, break off yarn, thread through rem sts and fasten off securely.

FINISHING

Join seam, reversing seam on rib for turnback.

Flora

A great project for any avid knitter who enjoys trying out
different stitches. A neat large tote bag, with a gusset and
self handles, knitted in Rowan *British Sheep Breeds DK*, it
has four different cables plus the addition of bobbles. The
yarn is springy, firm, and hard-wearing—just the thing for a
bag. To give it extra durability and strength, the bag has been
lined with a striped cotton fabric.

FINISHED SIZE
12in/30cm wide by 12½in/32cm deep.

YARN
6 x 1¾oz/131yd balls of Rowan *British Sheep Breeds DK* Bluefaced Leicester 780

NEEDLES
Pair of size 6 (4mm) knitting needles
Cable needle

EXTRAS
49in/125cm of 1½in/4cm wide petersham ribbon
Lining fabric, 20in/50cm by 1yd/1m
Batting, 20in/50cm by 1yd/1m

GAUGE
32 sts and 32 rows to 4in/10cm over patt using size 6 (4mm) needles *or size to obtain correct gauge.*

ABBREVIATIONS
MB—make bobble, [k1, p1, k1] all in next st, turn, k3, turn, p3, turn, k3, turn, then p3tog to complete the bobble.

C4B—cable 4 back, slip next 2 sts onto a cable needle and hold at back of work, k2, then k2 from cable needle.

C4F—cable 4 front, slip next 2 sts onto a cable needle and hold at front of work, k2, then k2 from cable needle.

C6B—cable 6 back, slip next 3 sts onto a cable needle and hold at back of work, k3, then k3 from cable needle.

Cr4R—cross 3 right, slip next st onto a cable needle and hold at back of work, k3, then p1 from cable needle.

Cr4L—cross 4 left, slip next 3 sts onto a cable needle and hold at front of work, p1, then k3 from cable needle.

Cr5R—cross 5 right, slip next 2 sts onto a cable needle and hold at back of work, k3, then p2 from cable needle.

Cr5L—cross 5 left, slip next 3 sts onto a cable needle and hold at front of work, p2, then k3 from cable needle.

See also page 133.

Cable Panel A (worked over 18 sts)
Row 1 (rs) P6, C6B, p6.
Row 2 K6, p6, k6.
Row 3 P4, Cr5R, Cr5L, p4.
Row 4 K4, p3, k4, p3, k4.
Row 5 P2, Cr5R, p4, Cr5L, p2.
Row 6 K2, p3, k8, p3, k2.
Row 7 P2, k3, p8, k3, p2.
Row 8 K2, p3, k8, p3, k2.
Row 9 P2, Cr5L, p4, Cr5R, p2.
Row 10 K4, p3, k4, p3, k4.
Row 11 P4, Cr5L, Cr5R, p4.
Row 12 K6, p6, k6.
These 12 rows form the pattern and are repeated.

Cable Panel B (worked over 14 sts)
Row 1 (rs) K1, p2, k8, p2, k1.
Row 2 P1, k2, p8, k2, p1.
Row 3 K1, p2, C4F, C4B, p2, k1.
Row 4 P1, k2, p8, k2, p1.
These 4 rows form the pattern and are repeated.

Cable Panel C (worked over 32 sts)
Row 1 (rs) P4, Cr4R, p5, C6B, p5, Cr4L, p4.
Row 2 K4, p3, k6, p6, k6, p3, k4.
Row 3 P3, Cr4R, p4, Cr5R, Cr5L, p4, Cr4L, p3.
Row 4 K3, p3, k5, p3, k4, p3, k5, p3, k3.
Row 5 P2, Cr4R, p3, Cr5R, p4, Cr5L, p3, Cr4L, p2.
Row 6 K2, p3, k1, MB, k2, p3, k8, p3, k2, MB, k1, p3, k2.
Row 7 P2, Cr4L, p3, k3, p8, k3, p3, Cr4R, p2.
Row 8 K3, p3, k3, p3, k8, p3, k3, p3, k3.
Row 9 P3, Cr4L, p2, Cr5L, p4, Cr5R, p2, Cr4R, p3.
Row 10 K4, p3, [k4, p3] twice, k4, p3, k4.
Row 11 P4, Cr4L, p3, Cr5L, Cr5R, p3, Cr4R, p4.
Row 12 K3, MB, k1, p3, k5, p6, k5, p3, k1, MB, k3.
These 12 rows form the pattern and are repeated.

BACK AND FRONT (both alike)
Using size 6 (4mm) needles, cast on 96 sts.
Foundation row (ws) K6, p6, k6, p1, k2, p8, k2, p1, k4, p3, k6, p6, k6, p3, k4, p1, k2, p8, k2, p1, k6, p6, k6.
Cont in patt.
Row 1 Work across 1st row of Cable Panels, A, B, C, B, and A.
Row 2 Work across 2nd row of Cable Panels A, B, C, B, and A.
These 2 rows set the position of the Cable panels.
Work a further 94 rows, ending with a row 12 on cable panels A and C.
Row 97 P6, * slip next 3 sts onto a cable needle and hold at back of work, [k next st tog with next st on cable needle] 3 times *, p6, patt 14, p4, Cr4R, p5, work from * to *, p5, Cr4L, p4, patt 14, p6, work from * to *, p6.
Row 98 K6, p3, k6, patt 14, p4, p3, k6, p3, k6, p3, k4, patt 14, k6, p3, k6.
Row 99 K15, patt 14, k29, patt 14, k15.
Rows 100 to 103 As row 99.
Next row Bind off 15 sts, patt next 13 sts, bind off 29 sts, patt next 13 sts, bind off rem 15 sts.
Straps
With right side facing rejoin yarn to first group of sts, cast on 6 sts, k these 6 sts, patt 14, cast on 6 sts. *26 sts.*
Row 1 (ws) P5, sl 1, patt 14, sl 1, p5.
Row 2 K6, patt 14, k6.
Rep the last 2 rows until strap measures 8in/20cm, ending with row 2 of cable panel.
Next row K7, p2, slip next 2 sts onto a cable needle and hold at front of work, [slip next st, k1 from cable needle, skp] twice, slip next 2 sts onto a cable needle and hold at back of work, [k next st tog with next st on cable needle] twice, p2, k7.
Next row P5, sl 1, p1, k2, p4, k2, p1, sl 1, p5.
Bind off.
With right side facing, rejoin yarn to second group of sts and work second strap as given for first.

GUSSET (make 2)

Using size 6 (4mm) needles, cast on 32 sts.

Row 1 K2, [work across row 1 of cable panel B] twice, k2.

Row 2 P2, [work across row 2 of cable panel B] twice, p2.

These 2 rows set the patt.

Cont in patt until gusset fits halfway along bottom edge and up side to row 96, ending with row 2 of cable panel.

Next row K3, p2, * slip next 2 sts onto a cable needle and hold at front of work, [slip next st, k1 from cable needle, skp] twice, slip next 2 sts onto a cable needle and hold at back of work, [k next st tog with next st on cable needle] twice *, p2, k2, p2; rep from * to *, p2, k3.

Next row P3, k2, p4, k2, p2, k2, p4, k2, p3.

K 5 rows.

Bind off.

FINISHING

Join cast-on edges of gusset. Using knitted pieces as a template and adding seam allowance, cut out front, back, sides, and base in batting and lining fabric. Baste batting to lining and use as one piece.

Join bound-off edges of handles.

Place petersham ribbon along center of wrong side of handle and slip stitch in place along knitted slipped sts. Bring row ends of handle together encasing petersham ribbon and sew row ends together to form seam.

Join cast-on edges of gusset.

With bound-off edges of gusset level with bound-off edges of sides, sew gusset to sides and cast-on edges of back and front, with seam at center of base.

Make up lining in same way. Place lining inside bag, fold seam allowance to wrong side, and slip stitch lining in place.

For extra stiffness in bottom of bag, cut a piece of cardboard to fit bottom. From lining make a "bag" to fit cardboard. Place in bottom of bag.

murray

A great unisex scarf with its mammoth 22-stitch double or horseshoe cable in a 24-row repeat, Murray is also knitted in Rowan *British Sheep Breeds Chunky* yarn, so despite being extravagantly long, it will knit up quickly. It makes an ideal project for a knitter new to cables. You can, of course, shorten it or knit it fashionably "super-long" as you wish.

ARAN KNITS

FINISHED SIZE
6½in/17cm wide by 62in/157cm long.

YARN
5 x 3½oz/120yd balls of *British Sheep Breeds Chunky* Bluefaced Leicester 950

NEEDLES
Pair of size 10½ (7mm) knitting needles
Cable needle

GAUGE
13 sts and 18 rows to 4in/10cm square over St st using size 10½ (7mm) needles *or size to obtain correct gauge.*

ABBREVIATIONS
C22B—cable 22 back slip next 11 sts on cable needle and hold at back of work, k11 then k11 from cable needle.
C22F—cable 22 front slip next 11 sts on cable needle and hold at front of work, k11 then k11 from cable needle.
See also page 133.

SCARF
Using size 10½ (7mm) needles, cast on 22 sts.
Row 1 K to end.
Row 2 P to end.
Break off yarn and leave these sts on a spare needle.
Using size 10½ (7mm) needles cast on 26 sts.
Row 1 (rs) P2, k22, p2.
Row 2 K2, p22, k2.
Rows 3 and 4 As rows 1 and 2.
Row 5 P2, k11, k22 from spare needle, k11, p2.
Row 6 K2, p44, k2.
Cont in patt.
Row 1 P2, k44, p2.
Row 2 K2, p44, k2.
Rows 3 to 20 Rep rows 1 and 2 nine times.
Row 21 P2, C22B, C22F, p2.
Row 22 As row 2.

Row 23 P2, k44, p2.
Row 24 K2, p44, k2.
These 24 rows form the patt.
Work a further 284 rows, ending row 20.
Row 309 P2, slip next 11 sts on cable needle and hold at back of work, [k next st tog with next st on cable needle] 11 times, slip next 11 sts on cable needle and hold at front of work, [k next st tog with next st on cable needle] 11 times, p2.
Row 310 K2, p22, k2.
Row 312 P2, k22, p2.
Bind off.

pattern information

SIZING

The instructions are given for the smallest size, and larger sizes follow in parentheses. If there is only one set of figures, it refers to all sizes. If - (hyphen) or 0 (zero) is given in an instruction for the size you are knitting, then that particular instruction does not apply to your size.

Included with each garment pattern in this book is a size diagram of the finished garment pieces and their dimensions. The size diagram shows the finished width of the garment at the underarm point, and it is this measurement that you should choose first; a useful tip is to measure one of your own garments that is a comfortable fit. Having chosen a size based on width, look at the corresponding length for that size; if you are not happy with the total recommended length, adjust your own garment before beginning your armhole shaping—any adjustment after this point will mean that your sleeve will not fit into your garment easily. Don't forget to take your adjustment into account if there is any side-seam shaping.

GAUGE

Obtaining the correct gauge can make the difference between a successful garment and a disastrous one. It controls both the shape and size of an article, so any variation from the pattern, however slight, can distort the finished garment.

You must match the gauge given at the start of each pattern. To check your gauge, knit a square in the pattern stitch and/or stockinette stitch of perhaps 5–10 more stitches and 5–10 more rows than those given in the gauge note. Press the finished square under a damp cloth and mark out the central 4in/10cm square with pins.

If you have too many stitches to 4in/10cm, try again using thicker needles. If you have too few stitches to 4in/10cm, try again using finer needles. Once you have achieved the correct gauge, your garment will be knitted to the measurements shown in the size diagram with the pattern.

CABLE PATTERNS

Cable stitch patterns allow you to twist the stitches in various ways, to create decorative effects such as an interesting rope-like structure to the knitting. The cables can be thin and fine (just a couple of stitches wide) or really big and chunky (up to 8 stitches wide or more).

To work cables, you need to hold the appropriate number of stitches that form the cable twist (abbreviated in pattern as C) on a separate small cable needle, while you knit behind or in front of them. You then knit the stitches off the cable needle before continuing to knit the remaining stitches in the row. Depending on whether the cable needle is at the front or the back of the work, the cables will twist to the left or right but the principle remains the same. A four-stitch cable will be abbreviated as C4F or C4B depending on whether the cable needle is held to the front or back of the work.

FINISHING METHODS
Pressing

Block out each piece of knitting by pinning it on a board to the correct measurements in the pattern. Then lightly press it according to the yarn label instructions, omitting any ribbed areas.

Take special care to press the edges, as this makes sewing up easier and neater. If you cannot press the fabric, then cover the knitted fabric with a damp cloth and allow it to stand for a couple of hours.

Darn in all ends neatly along the selvedge edge or a color join, as appropriate.

Stitching seams

When you stitch the pieces together, remember to match any areas of color and texture carefully where they meet. Use a special seam stitch, called mattress stitch, as it creates the neatest, flattest seam. After all the seams are complete, press the seams and hems.

Lastly, sew on the buttons to correspond with the positions of the buttonholes.

Making linings for bags

If you are knitting the bag in this book, it pays to line it carefully, using appropriate fabric. A good quality strong cotton is ideal for knitted bags as it provides some support for the fabric. Where the bag has a gusset at the base, you can add some extra strength to the base in the form of a cardboard liner, cut to the same size as the gusset. As you cannot wash the cardboard, you need to construct the liner for it so you can remove the cardboard easily.

It also pays to strengthen the straps of any bigger bags by wrapping the knitted pieces around a length of petersham ribbon, to make them less stretchy.

ABBREVIATIONS

The knitting pattern abbreviations used in this book are as below:

alt	alternate
approx	approximate
beg	begin(s)(ning)
cm	centimeters
cont	continu(e)(ing)
dec	decreas(e)(ing)
foll	follow(s)(ing)
garter st	garter stitch (K every row)
in	inch(es)
inc	increas(e)(ing)
K	knit
k2tog	knit next 2 sts together
m	meter(s)
M1	make one stitch by picking up horizontal loop before next stitch and knitting into back of it
M1pw	make one stitch by picking up horizontal loop before next stitch and purling into back of it
mm	millimeters
pw	purlwise
P	purl
patt	pattern
psso	pass slipped stitch over
p2sso	pass two slipped stitches over
p2tog	purl next 2 sts together
rem	remain(s)(ing)
rep	repeat
rev St st	reverse stockinette stitch
RS	right side
skp	sl 1, k1, psso
sl 1	slip one stitch
st(s)	stitch(es)
St st	stockinette stitch (1 row K, 1 row P)
tbl	through back of loop(s)
tog	together
WS	wrong side
yd	yard(s)
yo	yarn over

yarn information

The following are the specifications of the Rowan yarns used for the designs in this book. It is always best to try to obtain the exact yarns specified in the patterns, but when substituting yarns, remember to calculate the yarn amount needed by the yardage/meterage rather than by the ball weight. For yarn care directions, refer to the yarn label.

Rowan *Baby Alpaca DK*

A pure wool yarn (100 percent baby alpaca); 1¾oz/50g (approx 109yd/100m) per ball; 22 sts and 30 rows to 4in/10cm measured over St st using size 6 (4mm) knitting needles.

Rowan *British Sheep Breeds Chunky*

A medium weight pure British wool yarn; 3½oz/100g (120yd/110m) per ball; 13 sts and 18 rows to 4in/10cm measured over St st using sizes 10½–11 (7mm) knitting needles.

Rowan *British Sheep Breeds DK*

A pure British wool yarn; 1¾oz/50g (131yd/120m) per ball; 22 sts and 30 rows to 4in/10cm measured over St st using size 6 (4mm) knitting needles.

Rowan *Cashsoft 4 ply*

A lightweight wool/acrylic microfiber mix yarn (57 percent merino wool/33 percent acrylic microfiber/10 percent cashmere); 1¾oz/50g (approx 175yd/160m) per ball; 28sts and 36 rows to 4in/10cm measured over St st using size 3 (3.25mm) knitting needles.

Rowan *Felted Tweed*

A merino wool/alpaca/viscose mix yarn (50 percent merino wool/25 percent alpaca/25 percent viscose); 1¾oz/50g (191yd/175m) per ball; 22–24 sts and 30–32 rows to 4in/10cm measured over St st using sizes 5–6 (3.75–4mm) knitting needles.

Rowan *Felted Tweed Aran*

A merino wool/alpaca/viscose mix yarn (50 percent merino wool/25 percent alpaca/25 percent viscose); 1¾oz/50g (95yd/87m) per ball; 16 sts and 23 rows to 4in/10cm measured over St st using size 8 (5mm) knitting needles.

Rowan *Lima*

A sportweight baby alpaca/merino wool/nylon mix yarn (84 percent baby alpaca/8 percent merino/8 percent nylon); 1¾oz/50g (approx 109yd/100m) per ball; 20 sts and 26 rows to 4in/10cm measured over St st using size 9 (5.5mm) knitting needles.

Rowan *Wool Cotton*

A sportweight wool/cotton mix yarn (50 percent merino wool/50 percent cotton); 1¾oz/50g (approx 123yd/113m) per ball; 22–24 sts and 30–32 rows to 4in/10cm measured over St st using sizes 5–6 (3.75–4mm) knitting needles.

buying yarns

Rowan yarns (and buttons) have been used for all the knitting patterns in this book. See opposite for descriptions of the yarns used. To find out where to buy Rowan yarns near you, contact one of the Rowan yarn distributors given below. The main Rowan office is in the United Kingdom (see below for their website).

ROWAN YARN DISTRIBUTORS

USA
Westminster Fibers Inc, 8 Shelter Drive, Greer, 29650, South Carolina, 29650
Tel: (800) 445-9276
Email: info@westminsterfibers.com
www.westminsterfibers.com

UK
Rowan, Green Lane Mill, Holmfirth, West Yorkshire, HD9 2DX
Tel: +44 (0) 1484 681881
Email: mail@knitrowan.com
www.knitrowan.com

AUSTRALIA
Australian Country Spinners Pty Ltd, Level 7, 409 St. Kilda Road, Melbourne 3004.
Tel: 03 9380 3830
Email: tkohut@auspinners.com.au

AUSTRIA
Coats Harlander GmbH, Autokaderstrasse 31, Wien A-1210.
Tel: (01) 27716

BELGIUM
Coats Benelux, Ring Oost 14A, Ninove, 9400
Tel: 00 32 54 318989
Email: sales.coatsninove@coats.com

CANADA
See USA

CHINA
Coats Shanghai Ltd, No 9 Building, Baosheng Road, Songjiang Industrial Zone, Shanghai.
Tel: 86 21 5774 3733
Email: victor.li@coats.com

DENMARK
Coats HP A/S, Tagensvej 85C, St.tv., Copenhagen
Tel: 45 35 86 90 49
www.coatscrafts.dk

FINLAND
Coats Opti Crafts Oy, Ketjutie 3, Kerava, 04220
Tel: (358) 9 274871
Email: coatsopti@coats.com
wwwcoatscrafts.fi

FRANCE
Coats Steiner, 100 Avenue du Général de Gaulle, Mehun-Sur-Yèvre, 18500
Tel: 02 48 23 12 30
www.coatscrafts.fr

GERMANY
Coats GmbH, Kaiserstrasse 1, Kenzingen, 79341
Tel: 07162-14346
www.coatsgmbh.de

HOLLAND
See Belgium

HONG KONG
Coats Shanghai Ltd, No 8 Building , Export & Processing Garden, Songjiang Industrial Zone, Shanghai, China 201613
Tel: (86-21) 5774 3733

ICELAND
Rowan At Storkurinn, Laugavegur 59, Reykjavik, 101
Tel: 551 8258
Email: storkurinn@simnet.is
www.storkurinn.is

ISRAEL
Beit Hasidkit, Ms. Offra Tzenger, Sokolov St No 2, Kfar Sava, 44256
Tel: (972) 9 7482381

ITALY
Coats Cucirini srl, Viale Sarca n 223, Milano, 20126
Tel: (02) 636151
www.coatscucirini.com

KOREA
Coats Korea Co. Lt, 5F Eyeon B/D, 935-40 Bangbae-Dong, Seocho-Gu, Seoul, 137-060
Tel: 82-2-521-6262
www.coatskorea.co.kr

LEBANON
y.knot, Saifi Village, Mkhalissiya Street 162, Beirut
Tel: (961) 1 992211
Email: y.knot@cyberia.net.lb

LUXEMBOURG
See Belgium

MALTA
John Gregory Ltd, 8 TaíXbiex Sea Front, Msida, MSD 1512, Malta
Tel: +356 2133 0202
Email: raygreg@onvol.net

NEW ZEALAND
ACS New Zealand, 1 March Place, Belfast, Christchurch
Tel: 64-3-323-6665

NORWAY
Coats Knappehuset AS, Pb 100, Ulset, Bergen, 5873
Tel: 55 53 93 00

PORTUGAL
Coats & Clark, Quinta de Cravel, Apartado 444, Vila Nova de Gaia 4431-968
Tel: 223770700
www.crafts.com.pt

SINGAPORE
Golden Dragon Store, 101 Upper Cross Street, #02-51, Peopleís Park Centre, 058357, Singapore
Tel: (65) 65358454/65358234
Email: gdscraft@hotmail.com

SOUTH AFRICA
Arthur Bales Ltd, 62 Fourth Avenue, Linden, Johannesburg, 2195
Tel: (27) 118 882 401
Email: arthurb@new.co.za
www.arthurbales.co.za

SPAIN
Coats Fabra, SA, Santa Adria, 20, Barcelona, 08030
Tel: (34) 93 290 84 00
Email: atencion.clientes@coats.com
Web: www.coatscrafts.es

SWEDEN
Coats Expotex AB, JA Wettergrensgata 7, Vastra Frolunda, Goteborg, 431 30
Tel: (46) 33 720 79 00
www.coatscrafts.se

SWITZERLAND
Coats Stroppel AG, Turgi (AG), CH-5300
Tel: 056 298 12 20
www.coatscrafts.ch

TAIWAN
Cactus Quality Co Ltd, 7FL-2, No. 140, Sec. 2 Roosevelt Road, Taipei, Taiwan, R.O.C. 10084
Tel: 00886-2-23656527
Email:cqcl@ms17.hinet.net
www.excelcraft.com.tw

THAILAND
Global Wide Trading, 10 Lad Prao Soi 88, Bangkok 10310
Tel: 00 662 933 9019
Email: TheNeedleWorld@yahoo.com ñ global.wide@yahoo.com

For stockists in all other countries please contact Rowan for details

acknowledgments

AUTHOR'S ACKNOWLEDGMENTS

Martin Storey would like to specially thank: his nephew, Thomas Taylor, Laura Ramsey, and Ana Albulescu for being wonderful and patient models; Penny Hill and her team of knitters for the beautifully knitted designs featured in this book; Teresa Gogay for her invaluable help on knitting the swatches; Kate Buller, Marie Wallin, David Macleod, Lisa Richardson, and Ann Hinchcliffe at Rowan for their continuous support.

PUBLISHERS' ACKNOWLEDGMENTS

We would like to thank Anne Wilson for the design; John Heseltine for location photography; Ed Berry for still-life photography; Katie Hardwicke for editing; Penny Hill for pattern writing/knitting; Marilyn Wilson for pattern checking; Lisa Richardson for schematics; and Light Locations and the Golders Green Allotment Association (Carole Nolan in particular) for the locations for photography.